Housing Research Report

Barnsl

Private Landlords in England

Professor A D H Crook, Department of Town and Regional
Planning, University of Sheffield
and
Professor P A Kemp, Centre for Housing Research and Urban
Studies,
University of Glasgow.

London: HMSO

Department of the Environment

Recycled Paper

Contents

Acknowledgements

As always we have incurred many debts in carrying out the research presented in this report. The data presented in this report is based on two surveys of private landlords, one of which was funded by the Joseph Rowntree Foundation and the other by the Department of the Environment. We would like to thank the Joseph Rowntree Foundation for allowing the data from the survey which they funded to be incorporated into the present report. We are also grateful for the 813 landlords who participated in both surveys and agreed to be interviewed. The fieldwork was carried out Social and Community Planning Research with their usual efficiency and professionalism. Officials in the Department of the Environment gave us very helpful comments on our findings and on an earlier draft of the report. We are grateful to Phillip Lacey, our nominated officer in the Department, for his help and advice at all stages of the research. We would like to thank Margaret Johnson in the Centre for Housing Policy at the University of York (where Peter Kemp used to work) for her help and especially Joanne Gatensby for typesetting the report with her usual patience and skill.

Tony Crook and Peter A Kemp

1   Summary

Introduction

1.1   There is little up to date information about private landlords in England. The most recent national study was undertaken in 1982-1984, but only of the landlords who had made lettings during that period (Todd and Foxon, 1987). The last study of the landlords of a representative sample of all lettings in England was made as long ago as 1976, although it covered only lettings in areas where private renting households outnumbered owner occupiers (and also included housing associations in the study) (Paley, 1978).

1.2   Without more up to date information there is a risk that decisions made by policy makers, tenants, landlords, managing agents, and financial institutions will be based upon an understanding of the nature of private renting which no longer reflects current realities. Decisions will either be based upon out-of-date survey information or upon mythologies related to outdated or erroneous images of private landlords.

1.3   Collecting up-to-date information was, therefore, the reason for carrying out the first survey of landlords of a nationally representative sample of lettings in England for nearly two decades.

Private landlords in 1993-1994

1.4   The evidence about landlords in the 1990s comes from two surveys, carried out between December 1993 and September 1994, five years after rent deregulation came into effect in January 1989. This is a comparatively short time, coming after many decades of decline and net disinvestment, and it cannot be expected that there would inevitably be major changes in the structure of ownership or in the attitudes of landlords as a whole in such a short period. It will have taken some time for existing landlords to assess the significance for them of the changes made in 1989 and for any potential landlords to assess the new opportunities opened up by these changes and to act upon them.

Landlords

1.5   The structure of ownership was fundamentally similar to that found in earlier surveys. Although a wide range of individuals and organisations were letting accommodation, the ownership of the private rented sector was still dominated by individuals, each with only a small handful of lettings, often managed in their spare time. Moreover a greater proportion of lettings belonged to individuals than in earlier decades (and fewer to companies), although this was more a short term response to the owner occupied property slump than to fundamental long term changes in the structure of ownership, as individuals unable to sell their own houses let them out instead.

1.6   Sixty-one % of lettings were owned by individuals (or couples) and only 14% of these were full-time landlords. Only 20% were owned by companies,

1

including 11% that were owned by property companies (8% were residential property companies), and the remaining 19% were owned by partnerships and by organisations like churches, charitable trusts, Government departments and educational bodies, including universities. By comparison, 55% of all lettings in 1976 and 60% of lettings made between 1982 and 1984 were owned by individuals (Paley, 1978; Todd and Foxon, 1987).

1.7 Very few lettings, 17%, were owned by business landlords, those for whom letting accommodation was their core activity (that is, they were either full time individual landlords or property companies). A further 10% were owned by institutions (churches, Government departments, universities etc.). The remaining 73% were owned by sideline landlords: individuals, partnerships and companies for whom letting accommodation was not their main business.

1.8 Private renting was also mainly a small scale activity. A quarter of all lettings was owned by landlords who had only one letting. Fifty-five % of lettings had landlords who owned less than 10 lettings in all throughout England (the proportion in 1976 was 42%). The median size of all portfolios was only seven lettings. Eighty-eight % of lettings were parts of portfolios of less than 250: in other words were owned by landlords whose portfolios were the same as, or smaller than small housing associations (those with fewer than 250 lettings). Not surprisingly, therefore, very few lettings had landlords who depended upon rental income for more than a small part of their total income. For example 60% of lettings had landlords for whom rent was less than a quarter of their total income.

1.9 Private renting was still therefore very much a 'cottage industry'. Most of it was owned by sideline landlords and by landlords with few other lettings in total. As a result, most lettings had landlords who benefited neither from the scale economies nor risk diversification that can come with size. Under half the lettings were managed, in whole or in part, by managing agents. The latter tended to be responsible for routine tasks like rent collecting while landlords retained major decisions, like spending on repairs and whether to relet vacancies, for themselves.

1.10 Nearly a quarter, 24%, of all lettings were owned by 'new' landlords, those who had started letting accommodation in England for the first time during the five year period between rent deregulation in 1989 and the time of the surveys. This was broadly similar to the proportion, 20%, of all lettings owned in 1976 by those who had first started letting within the previous 6 years (Paley, 1978).

1.11 New landlords were more likely than continuing landlords to be sideline landlords, less likely to be business and institutional landlords, to have much smaller total holdings and less likely to regard their lettings as investments.

Acquiring lettings 1.12 While a substantial minority of all lettings and of recent lettings had been owned for many decades, the bulk had been acquired since 1979 (57% of all lettings and 61% of recent lettings). Moreover 32% of the recent lettings had been acquired since 1989, the year when all new lettings were deregulated, very similar to the proportion, 30%, of lettings made between 1982 and 1984, which had been acquired since 1980 (Todd & Foxon, 1987). Hence, there was a broadly similar pattern to the history of acquisitions, comparing lettings owned in 1993 and 1994 with those owned in earlier decades.

1.13 Like earlier decades, lettings had been acquired for a very diverse set of reasons, including to house employees and to help people out, as well as for investments. Thirty-seven % of all lettings and 38% of recent lettings had been acquired **mainly** for investment purposes (either for rental income or for capital gain), although this rose to about half when all reasons are taken into account. Thus it is clear that many landlords had not necessarily acquired lettings as investments, nor even in order to become landlords. The exception was business landlords. Over seven in 10 of lettings owned by them had been mainly acquired for investments.

1.14 Landlords had an equally diverse set of reasons for first letting the accommodation. Only 36% of all lettings had been first let either to provide an income (18%) or to provide a return on an investment (18%). This was the same as the proportion of lettings made between 1982 and 1984 which were considered to be investments when first let (Todd and Foxon, 1987). Many other reasons were important, such as providing housing for employees or getting help towards paying a mortgage.

1.15 Over three quarters of lettings had been purchased, rather than inherited or acquired in some other way. In most cases where lettings had been purchased, this had been with cash rather than with a loan: thus financial gearing in the private rented sector was very low and this was as true for lettings owned by business as by sideline landlords.

1.16 The majority of lettings had been acquired with vacant possession and most of these, 63%, had been acquired for letting, rather than to sell (which was 11%), or for landlords to occupy themselves (22%).

1.17 A difference between landlords in the 1990s and those in earlier decades, was the large proportion of lettings which had been let because they had once been the landlords' own homes which they had been unable or unwilling to sell because of the owner occupied property slump. About one in 10 of all lettings fell into this category, which was a large proportion of the flow of all new lettings made since deregulation. Whilst some of the flow of new lettings in past decades has always come from accommodation which was once their landlords' homes, the scale and reasons for the flow in the 1990s are very different from previous periods.

Attitudes to letting

1.18 While there were few differences in how landlords regarded their lettings in the 1990s compared with previous decades, landlords had much greater confidence about the business of letting in the 1990s than landlords had in the past.

1.19 Getting capital gains and, especially, rental income were seen as the good things about being a landlord, but providing accommodation for others and helping the local community were also mentioned as good things by a significant minority.

1.20 Repairs, arrears, troublesome tenants, getting repossession and the time taken up looking after property were most often mentioned as the worst things about being a landlord. Dealing with troublesome tenants was mentioned more than any other factor - by the landlords of 35% of lettings and by the agents of 56%.

1.21 However, most landlords and agents held positive rather than negative views about letting accommodation, especially business landlords, and this had increased significantly since the survey of landlords who had made lettings between 1982 and 1984.

1.22 For example, 67% of all lettings had landlords who agreed that the law allowed landlords to charge a reasonable level of rent, whereas only 39% of lettings made between 1982 and 1984 had landlords who agreed this (Todd and Foxon, 1987). Similarly the landlords of 46% of all lettings agreed that, on new lettings, landlords were adequately protected by the law against tenants refusing to leave. In 1982-1984 this proportion was only 17%.

1.23 The landlords of nearly half all lettings and the agents of over 80% said the situation had changed to the advantage of landlords since 1988 (because possession was easier, market rents could be charged and private renting had a better image). This was held more by business than by other landlords and more by those with larger than smaller portfolios.

1.24 Only a quarter of lettings had landlords (and the agents of 30% of lettings) who thought the situation had changed to their disadvantage. Significantly, the factors that had changed to their disadvantage included the greater competition between landlords when letting, compared with the situation before 1988, suggesting that a more competitive market had developed in the 1990s, with the balance of advantage swinging more towards tenants than landlords, compared with earlier periods. This was a marked change, compared with 1982-1984, when the proportion of lettings whose landlords thought matters had changed to their advantage in the previous six years was balanced by the proportion of lettings with landlords who thought matters had changed to their disadvantage.

Tenancy arrangements, the legal framework and letting strategies

1.25 Compared with 1982-1984, when 55% of lettings had landlords who said that it was better to let outside the Rent Acts, the surveys found that very few lettings were made by landlords using agreements not recognisable within the legal framework and which were designed to minimise tenants' security. In introducing assured shorthold tenancies, the 1988 Housing Act made it lawful for landlords to let short term tenancies at market rents and these had been used for most recent lettings made since deregulation. Assured tenancies had been used for comparatively few recent lettings.

1.26 An important finding of the surveys was that many landlords were not well informed about the legal framework for letting accommodation. For example, 25% of all lettings had landlords or agents who did not know the agreement they had let on, or described a type of agreement not recognised in law. This uncertainty or lack of knowledge is in fact largely confined to landlords, especially those with small portfolios. A third of all lettings had landlords in this position, compared with the agents of only five % of lettings.

1.27 Informal networks based upon personal contacts, rather than formal market-place techniques, like advertising, continued to be an important means of finding tenants in the 1990s (as they had been in earlier decades), especially where landlords, rather than agents, managed the lettings. However business landlords and sideline landlords who regarded their lettings as investments were more likely than others to use more formal methods of finding tenants. Landlords had been willing to negotiate with tenants about rents at only a small proportion of lettings. Landlords charged deposits or rent in advance at a large proportion of lettings, deposits and/or rent in advance having been charged at 86% of assured or assured shorthold lettings. This was broadly similar to earlier decades. For example, the landlords of 51% of lettings made between 1982 and 1984 had charged deposits, and 60% had charged rent in advance (Todd and Foxon, 1987).

1.28 Landlords and agents preferred to let to a wide range of household types when letting accommodation in the 1990s, but were least willing to let to young single people and households with children. They most preferred to let to those in work and least to students, the unemployed and others outside the labour market. Only small proportions of lettings had landlords and agents who said it was difficult to let to the types of tenants they most preferred.

Returns from letting

1.29 Direct comparisons between these and previous surveys are difficult to make (because some questions on the same topic were asked in different ways or not at all), the evidence suggests that landlords in the 1990s were more likely than before to say that their rents and returns were sufficient for their requirements.

1.30 Not all landlords charged rent. Twelve % of all lettings were rent free. Most landlords who charged rent, expected it to cover their costs, but, as previous surveys conducted in earlier decades had shown, only about 20%, expected it to provide them with a return (although a greater proportion of lettings owned by business landlords had owners who expected rents to provide a return).

1.31 However, compared with earlier decades, landlords in the 1990s who charged rent were more likely to say that it was sufficient. Half, 49%, of all lettings and 72% of recent lettings had landlords or agents who said that the rent on the most recent tenancy was sufficient to cover costs. In 1976 only 38% of lettings had landlords who thought the rent was 'adequate'. In 1993 nearly 59% of all tenancies made since deregulation had landlords who said that the rent was sufficient, but the proportion fell to 33% where the most recent tenancy had been made before deregulation.

1.32 Management and maintenance costs accounted for 30% of rent amongst all lettings and 26% of the rent amongst recent lettings. Arrears accounted for about 2% of rent due. Loss of rent because of voids accounted for two % of rent due amongst all lettings and six % of rent amongst recent lettings. Loss of rent from voids was particularly high amongst unfurnished lettings, suggesting that this was the area where competition between landlords for tenants was at its greatest.

1.33 The average gross rental yield (gross rents as a percentage of the landlords' estimate of vacant possession value) was 6.3% amongst all lettings and 8.4% amongst recent lettings. Gross yields were twice as high for lettings made since deregulation as for those made before then. Thus, amongst all lettings it was eight % for deregulated tenancies, compared with 3.6% amongst those let before deregulation.

1.34 Net rental yields averaged 5.5% amongst all lettings and 6.8% amongst recent lettings. Like gross yields, net yields were higher amongst deregulated lettings. They were 6.5% for all lettings made since deregulation, compared with 3.4% for those let before then.

1.35 Where landlords thought their rent was insufficient (47% of lettings), the rent they said would be sufficient implied a gross yield nearly four % higher than then being achieved. The average estimated sufficient gross yields were 10.2% amongst all lettings made since deregulation and 13.2% for recent lettings made since deregulation.

1.36 Where landlords were looking for a return from their total portfolio of lettings, half said that their rental income was sufficient to cover all repairs and give a reasonable return, although a half said that it was not. This was a significant change compared with earlier eras. In 1976, only 17% of lettings had landlords who said their total rent income was sufficient to cover repairs and give a return (Paley, 1978). Only 35% of landlords of lettings made between 1982 and 1984 said their total rent was sufficient (Todd and Foxon, 1987). Moreover, 60% of the lettings owned by business landlords in this survey had owners who thought their total rent income was sufficient.

Housing benefit   1.37 Private tenants had been able to get financial assistance with their rent before rent deregulation in 1988, but detailed information on landlords' attitudes towards the housing benefit system was not often collected in previous studies of landlords. This survey therefore provided important evidence for the first time from the landlords of a nationally representative sample of lettings about the extent to which their letting and rent setting policies were influenced by the Housing Benefit system.

1.38 Almost all landlords and agents had heard about Housing Benefit. Only about five % of lettings had landlords or agents who said they preferred to let to tenants on Housing Benefit. The majority preferred not to do so, although a large proportion had no preference either way. The reasons for preferring not to do so covered problems related to the administration of Housing Benefit, the precarious finances of tenants on benefit and the perception that tenants receiving it were 'undesirable'.

1.39 Nearly two fifths of lettings had landlords or agents with experience of rent officer referrals, for whom half had experience, on at least one occasion, of the rent being restricted. Only a minority took into account when setting their rent that it might be referred to Rent Officers for Housing Benefit purposes. Most disagreed that landlords could charge tenants on Housing Benefit a higher rent.

Landlords' difficulties and their sources of information

1.40 Whilst the survey evidence suggests that there have been important and positive changes in landlords' confidence in the legal framework for letting and in the returns they earn, the surveys found that landlords continued to have significant problems when letting accommodation. They also found that landlords continued, as in previous decades, to have difficulty finding out about how the law affected them.

1.41 Problems about arrears, difficult tenants, and regaining possession were the most common problems experienced by landlords and agents since 1988. A large proportion of landlords (especially those with larger than smaller portfolios) and agents sought advice about these and other problems, predominantly from solicitors, and most found the advice they got helpful.

1.42 Nearly all agents and half of all landlords had asked tenants to leave on at least one occasion since 1988, with arrears and unacceptable tenant behaviour (damage, noise, violence, abusive behaviour), being the main reasons. Thirty % of landlords and eight in 10 agents had taken court action at least once since 1988.

1.43 Landlords and agents used a very wide range of sources to get general information about letting, the most widely used being managing and estate agents, solicitors, reading statutes and property journals. Agents, business landlords and those who regarded their lettings as investments used far more sources than others. However, despite using this extensive range of information, only a minority of addresses, 44%, had landlords who disagreed with the view that it was hard to find out about how the law affected them. This is very similar to the proportion, 37%, of lettings made between 1982 and 1984, whose landlords said that they disagreed with this view (Todd and Foxon, 1987).

Likely future changes

1.44 Although most lettings would be relet if they became vacant, more lettings had landlords who expected a decrease rather than an increase in their total lettings, with the outcome depending upon what happens in the future to house prices as well as to rents.

1.45 Over 70% of lettings would be relet if they became vacant (compared with 40% in 1976). Where lettings would not be relet, this was not because of problems related to poor financial returns or to difficulties in managing property. Instead it was because of the many non-economic reasons why the accommodation had been let in the first place.

1.46 Most lettings, 59%, had landlords who did not expect their total portfolio to change in the next two years. Although 17% had landlords who expected to see an increase, 24% had owners who thought their total portfolio would decrease in size. These proportions are very similar to those found in the survey of landlords of lettings that were made between 1982 and 1984, although the proportion of lettings with landlords expecting a decrease is much smaller than the 46% found in 1976.

1.47 However whether or not landlords increase their total portfolio will depend upon future movements in both rents and house prices. The survey found it most likely that portfolios would increase if rents rose each year and house prices stayed the same. Thirty % of lettings had landlords who would increase lettings under this scenario. If rents fell and house prices rose, it was more likely that portfolios would fall in size: only 12% of lettings had landlords who would increase their portfolio under this scenario.

1.48 Lettings owned by business landlords and those regarding their letting as an investment were the most likely to be part of portfolios whose landlords expected their lettings to increase within two years and also expected to increase their lettings in response to specified house price and rent scenarios.

1.49 Landlords' future intentions will also be influenced by changes to Government policy. Getting easier repossession, having less troublesome tenants, charging higher rents and paying less tax were selected as the changes that would most help the landlords of nearly two thirds of lettings. Only 10% of lettings had landlords who said that Government subsidies or grants would most help, but those that said this were more likely to expect their portfolio to increase in size. Amongst all landlords, individual landlords said that paying less tax would be the most helpful financial assistance from Government. Company and other (non individual) landlords were more likely than individuals to select other forms of assistance, including grants and capital allowances.

Summary

1.50 The key points of this summary are that:

- there have not been major changes in the structure of the ownership of the private rented sector in England since rent deregulation;

- landlords have much greater confidence in the legal framework for letting in the 1990s, compared with earlier decades;

- although not all lettings had landlords who regarded their rent as sufficient, a greater proportion of lettings than in earlier decades have landlords who find rent income sufficient to cover their costs and give an adequate return;

- many landlords were still not well informed about the way the law affected them and many experienced significant problems when letting accommodation, especially over arrears, troublesome tenants and regaining possession;

- a greater proportion of lettings had landlords who expected their total holdings to decrease than to increase, but rising rents and falling house prices in the future could lead to an increase, rather than a decrease, in the stock of lettings owned by existing landlords.

2   Introduction

Background

2.1   Although increasing importance is being placed on the provision of accommodation by private landlords, relatively little systematic information is available about them. Most of the information that is available on the privately rented sector is about the tenants. For example, a succession of surveys has been carried out - in 1978, 1988, 1990 and 1993/94 - with national samples of private tenants (Todd, *et al.*, 1982; Dodd, 1990; Rauta and Pickering, 1992; Carey, 1995). In contrast, the most recent study of private landlords in England[†] was conducted over a decade ago, in 1982-84 as part of the Recent Private Lettings study commissioned by the Department of the Environment, which also included a survey of tenants (Todd and Foxon, 1987). It involved interviews with landlords who had taken out lettings during that period rather than with the stock of landlords as a whole. The last national study of private landlords as a whole was conducted two decades ago, in 1976 by OPCS on behalf of the Department of the Environment (Paley, 1978).

2.2   In the meantime, there have been very considerable changes in legislation and in the private letting environment more generally which may have had - and in the case of policy innovations were intended to have - an impact on the nature of private landlordism. So far as policy is concerned, the Housing Act 1980 introduced two new forms of tenancy - assured tenancies and shorthold tenancies - to supplement the regulated (Rent Act) tenancies which were then, in law, the main form of letting contract between landlord and tenant (the Appendix sets out a description of the key features of the different tenancy arrangements). Although at the time these new forms of tenancy had relatively little impact on the private lettings market (Crook, 1986; Kemp, 1988) they were subsequently amended by the 1988 Housing Act - which introduced assured and assured shorthold tenancies - which constitute the two principal forms of tenancies for new lettings.

2.3   The Housing Act 1988 deregulated all new lettings and made it easier for landlords to regain possession of their properties. It was hoped that allowing landlords to charge market rents would enable them to obtain a competitive return on their lettings and thereby stem or even reverse the long decline of the privately rented sector. Making it easier for landlords to regain possession was intended to increase the liquidity and reduce the risk of investment in residential property to let.

---

†   A survey of private landlords in Scotland, commissioned by Scottish Homes, was carried out i 1992/93 by Kemp and Rhodes (1994).

2.4   In addition to the 1988 Housing Act, several other measures were introduced to encourage investment (or discourage disinvestment) by private landlords. In November 1993 a new accelerated possession procedure was introduced to make it easier and quicker for landlords to evict tenants where the landlord has an irrefutable right to possession. The 1992 Budget introduced the 'rent a room scheme' under which resident landlords are exempt from income tax on rent up to the value of £3,250 per year.

2.5   Finally, the 1988 Budget extended the provisions of the Business Expansion Scheme (BES) to cover qualifying companies providing housing to let on assured tenancies. This extension of the scheme was intended to be temporary, applying until the end of 1993, and was made in order to provide what was referred to as a 'kickstart' to new investment in the sector. The BES provided substantial tax relief to individuals purchasing shares in BES assured tenancy companies and exemption from any capital gains on the sale of those shares provided they were held for at least five years. By the time the scheme came to an end in December 1993, over £3 billion had been invested in a total of approximately 900 BES assured tenancy companies, and around 81,000 homes were built or purchased from the money (Crook, Hughes and Kemp, 1995).

2.6   When the previous surveys of landlords were being carried out, the privately rented sector was declining in size, as indeed it had been since around the first world war. However, since 1988 the privately rented sector has expanded in size. The number of dwellings let privately increased by 14% between December 1988 and December 1993 (Down *et al.*, 1994).

2.7   It may be tempting to attribute this growth in private lettings to the measures introduced by the 1988 Housing Act and to the impact of the BES. However, these policy innovations were introduced at about the time when the owner occupied housing boom of the late 1980s came to a peak. Since then the owner occupied market has entered into a major recession. House prices have fallen in nominal as well as in real (ie, adjusted for inflation) terms; mortgage arrears and possessions have increased substantially; transactions have fallen; and an estimated million or so owners have found themselves with negative equity in the sense that the current market value of their home is less than the value of their outstanding mortgage (Forrest and Murie, 1994; Ford, Kempson and Wilson, 1995). The property slump has affected all regions of England but has been particularly severe in the South and in East Anglia.

2.8   The slump in the owner occupied housing market has affected both the demand for, and supply of, privately rented homes. There has been a growth of letting by home owners who are unable or unwilling at present to sell their former home because of the property slump, some of whom are themselves now renting accommodation from private landlords. At the same time, the evidence suggests that many young or new households who in the 1980s might have expected to buy their home are renting instead, for the time being at least. However, without the changes introduced by the Housing Act 1988, the number of owners who decided to let their former homes *pro tem* might have been much smaller than it has been.

2.9   Thus it is clear that the policy context and letting environment more generally has changed considerably since the earlier surveys of private landlords were carried out. For these reasons and because of the new policy emphasis on private renting, it was felt that there was a need for new, up to date information on the people and organisations who provide private accommodation to let. The social research division of the Department of the Environment therefore commissioned two research projects on private landlords[†]. In addition to this large scale, quantitative survey reported here, the Department commissioned SCPR conduct qualitative interviews with a sample of landlords. The results of the latter project were published in 1995 (Thomas and Snape, 1995).

Aims

2.10 The principal objective of this study was to obtain up to date, nationally representative, quantitative information about private landlords, either through direct interviews with landlords themselves or through interviews with their managing agents.

2.11 In particular, the research sought to examine:

- the sorts of people and organisations that become landlords and why they do so;
- the routes through which landlords enter the sector;
- the different tenancy arrangements which landlords enter into and their reasons for using them;
- landlords' and managing agents' understanding of the relevant legislative framework;
- the types of household which landlords and their agents prefer to have as tenants;
- the financial aspects of letting accommodation, including sources of finance, management and maintenance costs, and rates of return;
- the difficulties which landlords have experienced, including their experience of rent arrears, seeking possession and use of the courts;
- the sources from which landlords obtain their information about private letting and the information needs which they have;
- landlords' future intentions and the factors which might affect these intentions or influence their willingness to remain or invest further in the sector;
- landlords' views on possible policy innovations.

Methods

2.12 The research involved structured interviews with two samples of private landlords. The first sample survey was funded by the Joseph Rowntree Foundation (JRF) and the second by the Department of the Environment.

---

† In addition, the building stock research division of DoE commissioned a quantitative survey of the repair and renovation behaviour and views of private landlords (Crook, Heneberry and Hughes, 1996).

Preliminary results of the JRF funded survey - based on interviews with landlords in Britain rather than just in England - were included in a report on *The Supply of Privately Rented Homes* published by the JRF in March 1995 (Crook, Kemp and Hughes, 1995). The present report draws on both interview samples in order to facilitate a more detailed analysis of the data.

2.13 There is no readily available sampling frame for private landlords. The only feasible way of obtaining statistically reliable data about the people and organisations that let private housing is to obtain their names and addresses from a representative sample of private tenants. The JRF sample of landlord addresses was obtained from private tenants interviewed in the OPCS monthly Omnibus Survey; the sample for the DoE sample was obtained from tenants interviewed by OPCS in the Survey of English Housing. Both the Omnibus Survey and the SEH sample of households are drawn monthly by OPCS from the Postcode Address File. The subsequent interviews of landlords were conducted by SCPR using a questionnaire designed by the authors of this report.

2.14 In both samples, there were two separate but compatible versions of the questionnaire, one for landlords and the other for agents. There were minor wording differences to reflect the difference between the two types of respondent, but otherwise the questions were the same in both versions. However, the agent questionnaire was a shorter version of that used for the landlord interviews; questions which it was felt that agents would not necessarily be in a position to answer were excluded. The questionnaire used for both the JRF and the DoE samples were the same, except that ten additional questions - about difficulties, information needs, sources of advice, and court action - were added to the DoE one.

2.15 The questionnaires were in two parts. The first part comprised questions which were about a specific privately rented address, while the second part was made up of questions about the landlord's (or agent's) views and experience of letting accommodation more generally.

2.16 One crucial difference between the two surveys, however, was that only in the case of the JRF sample were the property specific questions asked about the privately rented address that had come up in the sample of tenants. In the DoE sample, because (as explained in the Appendix) the tenant was informed that their address would not be passed onto the survey firm, it was not possible to ask the landlord (or agent) about the sampled address; to get around this problem, landlords and agents were asked about the address at which they had made their most recent letting.

2.17 Because of this difference, it is possible to combine the data from the two surveys only in respect of the questions which were about the landlord's views and experiences in general and not those which were specific to the property. The property specific questions in the JRF survey are therefore based on a representative sample of privately rented addresses, while those in the DoE survey are based on the recent lettings of the landlords of a representative sample of privately rented addresses. We have referred to the former as the *all lettings* sample and the latter as the *recent lettings* sample.

2.18 In total 72% of Omnibus Survey private tenants gave information about their landlord; the remainder were either unwilling to pass on details or did not know their landlord's name or address. This yielded an unclustered sample of 600 names and addresses of landlords and agents. After removing addresses that proved to be out of scope, interviews were carried out in December 1993 and January 1994 with the landlords of 347 addresses in Great Britain (of which 301 were in England), a response rate of 75%. Of the landlord interviews in England, 212 (70%) were with landlords and 89 (30%)with managing agents.

2.19 In total, 65% of eligible SEH respondents provided information about their landlord in respect of 817 addresses. Interviews were subsequently carried out during August and September 1994 with the landlords of 547 privately rented addresses, a response rate (after excluding out of scope addresses) of 78%. Of these interviews, 334 (65%) were with landlords and 181 (35%) with agents.

2.20 Obtaining a sample of private landlords via private tenants in this way means that the survey provides information about *the landlords of a representative sample of privately rented addresses*. Hence the sample numbers used to calculate the percentages in the tables of the report are based on addresses and not on landlords. To illustrate this point, the figure of 61% in Table 2.1 should be read to mean that 61% of PRS addresses had a landlord that was a private individual; and not that 61% of landlords were private individuals. This distinction is important because many landlords own more than one letting. Hence if the tables had been calculated as a percentage of landlords it would mean that landlords with more than one letting would be under-represented in the data.

2.21 OPCS were commissioned by DoE to carry out a validation exercise to ascertain the representativeness of the achieved landlord sample derived from the SEH survey. The conclusion of this validation analysis was that there was little evidence of bias in the sample between tenants who provided landlord details and those who did not, between tenants whose landlord was interviewed and those whose landlord was not interviewed, and between landlords who were interviewed and those who were not.

3   Who are private landlords?

Summary

- a wide range of individuals and organisations were letting accommodation privately; but private landlordism was dominated by private individuals, who accounted for three out of five lettings, rather than corporate owners;

- two out of three lettings held by private individuals involved landlords who were in full-time or part-time employment; most of the remainder were either wholly retired or described themselves as full-time landlords;

- among lettings held by private individuals, 31% were owned by people aged 26 to 44, 40% by people aged 45 to 59, and 31% by people aged 60 or more;

- ninety-one % of lettings owned by private individuals were held by landlords who were white, whereas at the 1991 Census 96% of heads of household described their ethnic background as being white;

- eleven % of lettings were owned by property companies, including eight % which were owned by residential property companies;

- one in six lettings were owned by business landlords, three quarters by sideline landlords, and one in ten by institutional landlords;

- three out of five lettings were owned by landlords for whom rent accounted for a quarter or less of their income; for 70% of lettings owned by sideline landlords, rent was a quarter or less of their income; among just over half of lettings owned by business landlords, rent accounted for a half or more of their income;

- private lettings was a mainly small-scale activity: 26% of addresses were owned by landlords who had only one letting, and the median holding was only seven lettings; but 12% of landlords had 250 or more lettings and seven % had 1,000 or more;

- well under a half of lettings were managed in whole or in part by an agent on the landlord's behalf; agents were more likely to be responsible for the more routine tasks such as collecting rents and landlords more likely to retain responsibility for tasks which incurred expenditure (such as repairs) and those that were investment decisions (such whether to relet);

Introduction

3.1   This chapter presents a brief overview of some of the basic features of private landlords and provides the back cloth for the more detailed chapters which follow. It looks at: who lets private accommodation; whether private landlordism is a full-time business or sideline activity; the proportion of landlords' income that is accounted for by rent from residential lettings; the size of landlords' letting portfolios; and whether they make use of managing agents and for which tasks.

Types of landlord

3.2   The term 'private landlord' encompasses a wide range of types of individuals and organisations and includes some who would not recognise that term as a description of themselves. As Table 3.1 shows, three out of five (61%) of privately rented addresses were owned by private individuals or couples. Altogether a quarter were owned by partnerships (five %) and private (15%) or public (five %) companies. Another tenth were owned by institutions of one sort or another, including charities and charitable trusts (four %), the church and crown commissioners (one %), educational establishments (one %) and government departments (three %). The remainder (five %) were owned by a miscellany of organisations.

Table 3.1 : Type of landlord	
	%
Private individual/couple	61
Partnership	5
Private company	15
Public company	5
Charity or charitable trust	4
Church or Crown Commissioners	1
Government department	3
Educational establishment	1
Other	5
Total	**100**
(Base)	(811)
Base: all respondents	

3.3   The landlords of 69% of sampled addresses owned by private individuals were male, while 31% were female. Compared with heads of household in the general population, private landlords were very much less likely to be aged under 25 years and more likely to be middle aged or over 60 years old. Hardly any landlords were less than 25 years old, but three out of ten were aged between 25 and 44, four out of ten were between 45 and 59 years of age, and a little more than a quarter were aged 60 or more (Table 3.2).

Table 3.2 : Age of private individual landlords	%
Under 25	1
26 to 44	31
45 to 59	40
60 or over	27
Total	**100**
(Base)	(458)
Base: all private individual landlords	

3.4   Private individual landlords were more likely than the general population of heads of household to describe their ethnic background as other than white. According to the 1991 Census, 95.7% of heads of household were white; this compares with 90.7% of private individual landlords. The difference is accounted for by the relatively high proportion of private landlords who were of Indian, and to a lesser extent of Pakistani, ethnic background. Thus 4.3% of private individual landlords (Table 3.3) described their ethnic background as Indian compared with 1.1% of heads of household in the 1991 Census.

Table 3.3 : Ethnic background of private individual landlords	
	%
White	90.7
Black Caribbean	0.4
Black African	0.2
Indian	4.3
Pakistani	1.1
Bangladeshi	0.2
Chinese	0.4
Other	1.3
Refused/don't know	1.4
Total	**100**
(Base)	(460)
Base: all private individual landlords	

3.5   Over a third (37%) of private individual landlords said they did not have a paid job beside property management, while just under two thirds (63%) said they did have a job. Those who did not have a paid job were asked if managing property was their full-time job. Altogether, only about one in seven private individual landlords said managing property was their full-time job. Thus the majority of private individual owners were in effect part-time landlords; letting accommodation was a spare time activity and not their main occupation. As Thomas and Snape (1995) have described them, they were 'sideline' landlords.

3.6   Among lettings held by private individuals, 51% were in full-time work, defined as being 30 hours or more a week. Another 12% were either in part-time work or had hours of work that varied from one week to the next. And 16% private individuals described themselves as being wholly retired (Table 3.4).

Table 3.4 : Work status of private individual landlords	
	%
Full-time landlord	14.5
Paid employment 30+ hours pw	51.4
Paid employment less than 30 hours pw/hours vary	12.2
Looking for work	1.3
Temporarily sick	0.3
Long-term sick/disabled	0.6
Wholly retired	16.1
Looking after home/family	2.9
Other	0.6
Total	**100**
(Base)	(311)

Base: private individual landlords

3.7   The owners of privately rented accommodation who were not private individuals are described in this report as corporate landlords. This includes partnerships, companies, charitable trusts and various types of institution such as health authorities. One in five sampled addresses were owned by companies, of which three quarters were private and one quarter were public companies (Table 3.1). Not all companies were mainly involved in letting property. Just under three out of five (58%) addresses held by companies were owned by property companies, of which three quarters were mainly concerned with residential property. One in seven of the addresses held by residential property companies were owned by business expansion scheme firms. Thus 11% of all privately rented addresses were owned by property companies, including eight % that were owned by residential property companies.

3.8   Combining property companies with the private individual landlords who were involved full-time in letting accommodation, one in six (16.9%) of privately rented addresses were owned by what were in effect full-time landlords. Hence, for these landlords, property was their core business. They very broadly conform with the description of 'business landlords' discussed in the DoE's qualitative study of private landlords (Thomas and Snape, 1995). A further one in 10 (9.5%) addresses were owned by various types of institution. The remaining three quarters of addresses (73.7%) were owned by what, to use Thomas and Snape's terminology, could be described as sideline landlords; that is to say, they were neither full-time landlords as defined above nor institutions. These three types of landlord are shown in Table 3.5.

Table 3.5 : Privately rented addresses by type of landlord	
	%
Business landlord	17
Sideline landlord	74
Institutional landlord	10
All landlords	**100**
(Base)	(811)

Rent as income 3.9   Table 3.6 shows that the majority of addresses were owned by private landlords for whom rent from residential lettings accounted for a minority share of their income. Sixty % of addresses were owned by landlords for whom rent accounted for up to a quarter of their income. Only 12% of addresses were owned by landlords for whom residential rent was three quarters or more of their income. For 20% of addresses, rent accounted for between a quarter and three quarters of the landlord's income. Thus while rent was, if not the main, then at least a substantial contributor to the incomes of the landlords of a substantial minority of privately rented addresses, for most it was a minority source of revenue. This confirms the fact that the majority of addresses were owned by people and organisations for whom private landlordism was not their primary source of livelihood.

Table 3.6 : Rent as a proportion of income by type of landlord	Business landlords	Sideline landlords	Institution	All landlords
	%	%	%	%
Up to 25%	24	70	62	60
26 to 50%	19	13	2	13
51 to 75%	21	4	2	7
76 to 100%	33	6	13	12
Don't know/refused	4	7	22	8
Total	**100**	**100**	**100**	**100**
(Base)	(102)	(370)	(55)	(527)
Base: all landlords				

3.10 There were significant differences between business, sideline and institutional landlords in respect of the share of their income that was from residential rents. Among addresses held by sideline landlords, 70% had an owner for whom rent was a quarter or less of their income, compared with only

24% of business landlords and 62% of institutional landlords. Conversely, 33% of addresses held by business landlords, compared with only six % held by sideline landlords and 13% held by institutional landlords, had an owner for which rent accounted for more than three quarters of their income. For 53% of addresses held by business landlords, rent from residential lettings accounted for half or more of the owner's income; among lettings held by sideline landlords only 10%, and among lettings held by institutional landlords only 15%, were receiving half or more of their income in rent (Table 3.6).

Portfolio size

3.11 As well as being a mainly part-time or sideline activity, letting residential property was also for the most part a small scale operation. The median size of portfolio was only seven lettings. A quarter of addresses were owned by landlords with just one letting, while three quarters were owned by landlords who had 40 or less lettings. There was, however, a very wide variation around the median, ranging from one letting at one extreme to 90,000 at the other. The largest owners were more likely to be the institutional landlords rather than private or public companies.

3.12 A quarter of all privately rented addresses were owned by landlords who had only one letting. Just over half of all addresses were owned by landlords who had less than 10 lettings in total. At the other extreme, about one in 10 addresses were owned by landlords who had 500 or more lettings. Approximately one in six addresses were owned by landlords who had 100 or more lettings (Table 3.7).

Table 3.7 : Size of lettings portfolio

	Private individual landlords	Corporate landlords	All landlords
	%	%	%
1	43	3	26
2 - 4	23	8	17
5 - 9	15	8	12
10 - 24	12	18	14
25 - 49	5	11	7
50 - 99	2	9	5
100 - 249	2	13	6
250 - 499	-	8	3
500 - 999	-	6	2
1000+	-	16	7
Total	**100**	**100**	**100**
(Base)	(308)	(214)	(527)

Base: all landlords

3.13 Not surprisingly, larger portfolios were owned by corporate landlords and smaller ones by private individuals. Thus 43% of addresses held by private individuals were owned by people who had only one letting, 66% by people who had less than five lettings, and 82% by people who owned less than 10 lettings. Nine % of addresses were held by private individual landlords who had a stock of 25 or more lettings.

3.14 Among addresses owned by corporate landlords, 19% were held by landlords who had a portfolio that was of less than 10 lettings in size, and 37% by landlords with a portfolio of less than 25 lettings. At the other extreme, 43% of addresses let by corporate landlords were owned by organisations with a portfolio of 100 or more lettings. And 16% of addresses owned by corporate landlords involved organisations that had stocks of 1,000 or more lettings.

3.15 There were significant differences between business, sideline and institutional landlords in respect of portfolio size. Thirty-seven % of addresses held by sideline landlords had owners with just one letting. Indeed, almost all (98%) of lettings where the owner had just one letting were sideline landlords. Forty-two % of five addresses held by business landlords had owners in the upper quartile (41 or more lettings) in terms of portfolio size; this was also the case for 69% of addresses held by institutional landlords and only 14% of addresses owned by sideline landlords (Table 3.8).

Table 3.8 : Size of lettings portfolio by type of landlord				
	Business landlords	Sideline landlords	Institutions	All landlords
	%	%	%	%
1 letting	3	37	-	27
2 to 7 lettings	19	29	10	25
8 to 40 lettings	36	21	21	24
41 or more lettings	42	14	69	25
Total	**100**	**100**	**100**	**100**
(Base)	(100)	(369)	(52)	(521)
Base: all landlords				

Use of managing agents

3.16 The majority of privately rented addresses were managed solely by the landlord, without the help of an agent. There was, however, a statistically significant difference between the sample of lettings for the sector as a whole and the sample of the most recent lettings made by landlords of those addresses. Across the sector as a whole, 64% of lettings were managed solely by the landlord and 37% partly or in whole by an agent. Among the most recent lettings made by landlords, 56% were managed by the landlord alone and 44% wholly or in part by an agent. Thus recent lettings are more likely than the sector as a whole to be managed by an agent.

3.17 Addresses which were owned by private individuals were more likely than the average, and those which were owned by companies and by institutions were less likely than the average, to be managed by an agent. Business landlords were less likely, and sideline landlords more likely, than the average to be using an agent. There were no statistically significant differences by portfolio size in the usage of managing agents.

3.18 In the DoE's qualitative study of private landlords, it was found that managing agents tended to be employed most often when the property was located some distance away from the landlord's own home. This was particularly true of sideline landlords, including those who had become involved in letting as a result of the property slump. Business landlords who undertook the management themselves felt that managing agents would not look after the property as well as they would (Thomas and Snape, 1995).

3.19 Where landlords did make use of an agent, the division of labour between the landlord and the agent varied according to the particular task (Table 3.9). The task that was most likely to be devolved to the managing agent was deciding the rent level: in three quarters of addresses where the management was contracted out, the landlord left this to the agent. Agents were much more likely than landlords to be responsible for collecting the rent and for selecting the tenants; that is, for the more every day tasks of property management.

Landlords were more likely to keep responsibility for deciding on minor repairs and maintenance, whether to relet a vacancy, and deciding on major repairs and improvements; all of them tasks that involved the expenditure of money (minor repairs, major repairs) or were investment decisions (whether to relet, major repairs). In some cases - especially deciding on major repairs, selecting tenants and deciding whether or not to issue a notice to quit - the landlord shared the task with the agent.

Table 3.9 : Division of management tasks where the landlord uses an agent		Landlord	Agent	Jointly	Total	(Base)
Collects the rent	%	31	69	-	100	(108)
Negotiates rent levels	%	18	74	8	100	(108)
Selects tenants	%	10	67	23	100	(108)
Decides to give Notice to Quit	%	43	36	21	100	(106)
Decides whether to re let a vacancy	%	63	19	18	100	(110)
Decides on minor repairs and maintenance	%	55	35	11	100	(110)
Decides on major repairs and improvements	%	71	4	26	100	(110)

3.20 The great majority of landlords who used an agent were satisfied with the service they received. Thus, the landlords of a quarter (25%) of addresses where an agent was employed expressed themselves to be fairly satisfied with the service and three fifths (63%) said they were very satisfied with it. Only one in 13 (eight %) said they were dissatisfied with the service that their agent gave them.

3.21 The DoE's qualitative study of private landlords found that, where landlords were dissatisfied with the service they got from the agent, the main problem was a perceived lack of communication. For example, in some cases the landlord had specified that they would prefer the accommodation to be let to one category of tenant (such as professional people) but the agent had let it to other categories (such as students or people on Housing Benefit). The study also found that, while some landlords were satisfied and others were dissatisfied with the service provided by the agent, there was a general feeling that the fees charged were high for the work carried out (Thomas and Snape, 1995).

4   Acquisition and first letting

Summary

- while a substantial minority of property in both samples had been owned by the landlord for many decades, the bulk of lettings had been acquired since 1979;

- landlords had diverse reasons for acquiring the letting. Only two fifths of both samples had been mainly acquired for investment (rental income or capital gain) purposes; this rises to about half when all reasons are taken into account as for some landlords it was a secondary factor;

- the majority of lettings in both samples had been acquired by the landlord buying the property, in most cases for cash rather than with a loan; around one in six lettings had been inherited;

- the majority of lettings had been acquired so the landlord could let the property rather than sell or occupy it;

- the majority of lettings had been acquired with vacant possession;

- a substantial minority of lettings were not first let in the year the landlord acquired the property; the average gap between acquisition and first letting was five years;

- seven out of 10 lettings were first let by the landlord after 1979; four out of 10 lettings had been first let by the landlord after 1988;

- landlords had diverse reasons for first letting the accommodation; less than half had done so mainly for investment reasons;

Introduction

4.1   This chapter examines the property acquisition process and the decision to start letting the accommodation to tenants. It explores these questions in respect of the sampled address in the case of the all lettings sample, and the property at which the most recent letting was made by the landlord or agent in the most recent lettings sample. In particular it examines when the accommodation was acquired; the reasons why it was acquired; how it had been acquired; when landlords had first let the accommodation; and the reasons why they had done so.

Date of acquisition

4.2   Landlords and agents were asked when the landlord had first acquired the property; in the case of the first sweep of interviews, this referred to the sampled privately rented address ('all lettings'); in the case of the second sweep of interviews, it referred to the most recent letting ('most recent lettings') made by the landlord or agent. About one in five respondents in both samples did not know (or could not recall) when the address had been acquired by the landlord; perhaps not surprisingly, the great majority (86%) of these respondents were agents.

4.3   Table 4.1 shows the date at which the address had been acquired leaving aside those who did not know. The differences between all lettings and most recent lettings were not statistically significant. A quarter of all lettings and a third of the most recent lettings had been acquired since rents were deregulated in January 1989. About three fifths of both had been acquired since 1979 and one in seven of all lettings and one in 10 of most recent lettings had been acquired before 1945. Conversely, one in five and one in six respectively had been acquired before 1957. Thus, while a substantial minority had been owned by the landlord for many decades, the bulk of both all lettings and most recent lettings had been acquired relatively recently.

4.4   Within each of the two categories of lettings, there were significant differences in the date of acquisition by type of landlord (Table 4.2). Among the sample of all lettings, the main difference was between those owned by institutional landlords on the one hand and business and sideline landlords on the other. Lettings owned by institutional landlords were more likely to have been acquired before 1957 and less likely to have been acquired after 1980. This age profile of lettings owned by institutions is repeated among the sample of the most recent lettings. However, among the recent lettings sample, those owned by sideline landlords were more likely than those owned by business landlords to have been acquired since 1980 and since 1989.

Table 4.1 : Year landlord acquired the address		
	All lettings	Most recent lettings
	%	%
Before 1945	14	10
1945 to 1956	5	6
1957 to 1964	6	5
1965 to 1979	18	20
1980 to 1988	33	29
1989 to 1994	24	32
Total	100	100
(Base)	(249)	(430)

Table 4.2 : Year landlord acquired the address by type of landlord						
	All lettings			Most recent lettings		
	Business	Sideline	Institution	Business	Sideline	Institution
	%	%	%	%	%	%
Before 1945	14	14	15	10	8	26
1945 to 1956	5	3	22	9	4	14
1957 to 1964	5	7	7	11	3	5
1965 to 1979	24	15	26	26	18	19
1980 to 1988	24	37	19	20	33	16
1989 to 1994	29	24	11	24	35	21
Total	**100**	**100**	**100**	**100**	**100**	**100**
(Base)	(42)	(180)	(27)	(80)	(307)	(43)

Reasons for acquiring the address

4.5   Landlords had a diverse range of reasons for acquiring the property. The differences between the all lettings and the most recent lettings sample were not statistically significant. Twenty-nine % of all lettings and 33% of the most recent lettings had been acquired as an investment for rent, while 28% and 23% respectively had been acquired as an investment for capital gain. Twenty-one % of all lettings and 26% of the most recent lettings had been acquired for the landlord to live in at some stage, not necessarily at the time of purchase. Six % of both samples had been acquired so that the landlord could help someone out (in a third of these cases the property was let to a relative), while two % and three % respectively had been acquired for charitable reasons. Thirteen % of all lettings and 11% of the most recent lettings has been acquired in order to house an employee. Eleven % of both samples had been inherited or received as a gift. In five % and seven % of cases respectively, the letting had been acquired as an incidental part of a wider purchase (such as a flat over a shop or a cottage with a farm).

4.6   In both samples approximately a third of landlords had more than one reason for their acquisition of the property. Table 4.3 shows the single *most important* reason why the landlord had acquired the property. Altogether only about two fifths of lettings in both samples had been acquired mainly for investment purposes. However, when *all* reasons (not just the most important one) are taken into account, investment purposes were mentioned in respect of about half of all addresses in both of the samples. Thus it is clear that people and organisations did not necessarily acquire the accommodation for investment purposes nor even in order to become landlords.

4.7   In the recent lettings sample, there were statistically significant differences between 'new' landlords (those who had acquired all of their lettings portfolio after January 1989) and 'continuing landlords' (those who had acquired all or some of their lettings before 1989). New landlords were less likely than continuing landlords to mention investment as the main reason why they had acquired the address (20% compared with 35%). On the other hand, new landlords were very much more likely than continuing ones to say they acquired the address in order to live there (41% compared with 13%). A similar pattern existed in the all lettings sample but the differences were not statistically significant.

Table 4.3 : Main reason why landlord acquired the address		
	All lettings	Most recent lettings
	%	%
As an investment for rental income	17	25
As an investment for capital growth	20	13
To live in (at some time)	14	15
To help someone out	5	5
To house an employee	15	10
For charitable reasons	1	3
Incidental to another transaction	6	9
Inherited/gift	10	10
Other reason	12	10
Total	**100**	**100**
(Base)	(212)	(327)

4.8   Within both samples, there were statistically significant differences between the three landlord types - business, sideline, and institution - in their main reason for acquiring the property (Table 4.4). In both samples, business landlords were very much more likely than either of the other types of landlord to have acquired the letting for investment purposes, whether this was for the rental income or capital gain. Thus 75% of all lettings, and 71% of most recent lettings, owned by business landlords had been mainly acquired either for rental income or for capital growth.

4.9   By contrast, institutional landlords were much less likely than either of the other types of landlord to have acquired the property for either of these reasons; instead, they were very much more likely to have acquired the property to house an employee. Thus 49% of all lettings, and 42% of most recent lettings, owned by institutions had been acquired in order to house an employee. In both samples 14% had been acquired by an institution for charitable reasons, whereas none of the lettings owned by business landlords and hardly any of those owned by sideline landlords in either sample had been mainly acquired for that reason (Table 4.4).

4.10 A fifth of lettings owned by sideline landlords in both samples had been acquired mainly in order for the owner to live in the property at some stage. None of the institutional landlords had acquired the property in either sample for this reason; this was also true of all business landlords in the all lettings sample and all but a few of them in the most recent lettings sample (Table 4.4).

Table 4.4 : Main reason why landlords acquired the address by type of landlord	All lettings			Most recent lettings		
	Business	Sideline	Institution	Business	Sideline	Institution
	%	%	%	%	%	%
As an investment for rental income	40	12	5	52	21	8
As an investment for capital growth	35	19	-	19	13	3
To live in (at some time)	-	20	-	3	21	-
To help someone out	3	6	-	2	7	3
To house an employee	3	13	50	2	8	42
For charitable reasons	-	-	14	-	2	14
Incidental to another transaction	-	6	14	5	10	6
Inherited/gift	15	11	-	11	11	3
Other reason	5	13	18	6	8	22
Total	**100**	**100**	**100**	**100**	**100**	**100**
(Base)	(40)	(150)	(22)	(63)	(228)	(36)

How the letting had been acquired

4.11 In both of the samples, just over three quarters of lettings had been bought by the landlord for cash or with a loan (Table 4.5). In the landlord interviews (but not the ones with their agents) it was possible to explore property acquisition in more detail. The differences between the two samples were not statistically significant. Among the *landlords* who were interviewed, by far the most common mode of acquisition in both samples was purchase by cash: 49% of the all lettings sample and 42% of the most recent lettings sample of properties had been bought in this way. In the all lettings sample 13% had been purchased with the help of a loan, as had 21% in the recent lettings sample. Fifteen % of addresses in the all lettings sample and 18% in the recent lettings sample had been inherited, according to the landlords who were interviewed, while four % and three % respectively had been received as a gift (Table 4.5).

Table 4.5 : How the letting had been acquired	All lettings	Most recent lettings
	%	%
Bought with cash	49	42
Bought with a loan	13	21
Inherited	15	18
Received as a gift	6	4
Acquired the organisation that previously owned it	4	3
Some other way	10	11
Don't know	3	3
Total	**100**	**100**
(Base)	(154)	(238)

4.12 There were significant differences within the two samples in the way in which the letting had been acquired, mainly between business and sideline landlords on the one hand and institutional landlords on the other. In both samples none of the institutional landlords said they had purchased the letting with a loan, while a significant minority of business and sideline landlords had done so. Whereas business and sideline landlords were much more likely than institutional landlords to have inherited the letting, institutions were more likely than the other two types of landlord to have received it as a gift (Table 4.6).

4.13 Landlords who had purchased the letting were asked whether they had done so in order to let it, to sell it, or to occupy it themselves. The overall differences between the two samples were statistically significant. In both samples, the majority of lettings had been acquired by the landlord in order to be let to tenants: 63% of all lettings and 65% of most recent lettings had been acquired for this purpose. However, in the all lettings sample, more property had been acquired in order to sell and less in order to self-occupy than among the most recent lettings sample (Table 4.7).

4.14 There were no statistically significant differences between new and continuing landlords in respect of how they had acquired the address, but there were in whether they had acquired the letting in order to sell, let or occupy it. In both samples, new landlords were much less likely than continuing ones to have acquired the address in order to let it and much more likely to have acquired it in order to live there. Thus in the all lettings sample, 41% of new landlords compared with 68% of continuing ones had acquired the address in order to let it to tenants; in the recent lettings sample, 39% of new and 74% of continuing landlords had acquired the address primarily for that reason. In the all lettings sample, 48% of new landlords compared with 18% of continuing landlords had acquired the address in order to live there; in the recent lettings sample, the figures were 52% and 21% respectively.

Table 4.6 : How the letting had been acquired by type of landlord						
	All lettings			Most recent lettings		
	Business	Sideline	Institution	Business	Sideline	Institution
	%	%	%	%	%	%
Bought with cash	47	50	52	39	42	45
Bought with a loan	13	16	-	26	23	-
Inherited	19	17	-	15	21	7
Received as a gift	3	5	14	6	3	10
Acquired the organisation that previously owned it	13	2	-	-	4	-
Some other way	6	9	24	13	5	35
Don't know	-	2	10	2	3	3
Total	**100**	**100**	**100**	**100**	**100**	**100**
(Base)	(32)	(101)	(21)	(54)	(155)	(29)

Table 4.7 : Whether landlords who had purchased the address had done so in order to let, to sell, or to occupy it		
	All lettings	Most recent lettings
	%	%
To let	63	65
To sell	11	4
To occupy	22	29
Can't say	4	2
Total	**100**	**100**
(Base)	(161)	(254)

4.15 Once again, there were significant differences within both of the samples. Lettings held by institutions were more likely than those held by the other two types of owner (especially sideline landlords) to have been purchased for letting. Lettings owned by sideline landlords were much more likely than those owned by the other types of landlord to have been acquired for self-occupation. Finally, lettings owned by business landlords (most especially those in the all lettings sample) were much more likely than those owned by the others to have been bought in order to sell (Table 4.8). In almost all cases where the letting had been bought in order to sell (not necessarily immediately after purchase) the intention had been to sell it with vacant possession rather than with sitting tenants, presumably in anticipation of capital gain.

Table 4.8 : Whether landlords who had purchased the address had done so in order to let, to sell or to occupy it, by type of landlord

	All lettings			Most recent lettings		
	Business	Sideline	Institution	Business	Sideline	Institution
	%	%	%	%	%	%
To let	68	59	81	83	57	90
To sell	26	8	-	8	3	-
To occupy	3	30	6	8	36	11
Can't say	3	4	13	-	3	-
Total	**100**	**100**	**100**	**100**	**100**	**100**
(Base)	(31)	(114)	(16)	(48)	(187)	(19)

4.16 According to both the landlords and the agents who were interviewed, the majority of lettings in both samples were acquired with vacant possession; this was especially true of the most recent lettings sample (Table 4.9).   Over a third of the sample of all lettings, and a quarter of the most recent lettings sample, had been acquired with sitting tenants. New landlords were much more likely than continuing ones to have acquired the sampled address vacant and less likely to have acquired it with sitting tenants.

Table 4.9 : Whether landlords had acquired the address with vacant possession or already let to tenants

	All lettings	Most recent lettings
	%	%
Vacant	56	70
Partly let	3	6
Wholly let	33	19
Don't know	8	6
Total	**100**	**100**
(Base)	(292)	(506)

4.17 There were significant differences once again within the two samples. Among both all lettings and most recent lettings, those owned by institutions were more likely than the others to have been acquired vacant. In both samples, those owned by business landlords were much more likely to have been acquired with sitting tenants; this was especially true of the all lettings sample, of which over three fifths of those owned by business landlords had been acquired with tenants already living in them (Table 4.10). Thus whereas the majority of the all lettings sample that was owned by sideline and especially by institutional landlords was acquired vacant, the majority of lettings owned by business landlords were acquired tenanted.

Table 4.10 : Whether landlords had acquired the address with vacant or already let to tenants, by type of landlord						
	All lettings			Most recent lettings		
	Business	Sideline	Institution	Business	Sideline	Institution
	%	%	%	%	%	%
Vacant	29	59	81	51	73	78
Partly let	2	4	-	12	5	2
Wholly let	61	30	12	29	17	17
Don't know	8	7	8	8	6	26
Total	**100**	**100**	**100**	**100**	**100**	**100**
(Base)	(49)	(217)	(26)	(85)	(375)	(46)

4.18 Addresses that were inherited or had been received as a gift were much more likely than other addresses to have been acquired with sitting tenants. Thus in the all lettings sample, 77% of inherited addresses had been acquired with sitting tenants compared with 42% of non inherited addresses. In the recent lettings sample, 61% of inherited addresses had been acquired with tenants compared with 22% of non inherited addresses.

Year the landlord first let the accommodation

4.19 The properties were not all first let in the same year that they had been acquired, though the majority had been. Thus 63% of the all lettings sample and 55% of the most recent lettings sample had been let in the same calendar year as that in which the letting had been acquired. Twenty-five % and 26% respectively had been first let between one and five years of the date in which the letting had been acquired. Eleven % and 19% respectively had been first let six or more years after acquisition (the longest gap was 54 years). The average gap for both samples was five years. Among business landlords, the average gap between purchase and first letting for both samples was three years; among sideline landlords it was four years in the all lettings sample and five in the most recent lettings sample. Among institutional landlords it was nine years and 10 years respectively.

4.20 As a result of these gaps, in both samples the age profile of first letting was more recent than that for when the property was acquired (compare Table 4.11 with Table 4.1). In the case of 13% of all lettings and 10% of most recent lettings, the landlord or agent did not know or could not remember when the property had first been let by the present owner; it seems plausible to suppose that the age profile of first letting of these don't knows was older than that of lettings where the landlord or agent did know when it was first let by the present owner.

Table 4.11 : Year landlords first let the accommodation	All lettings	Recent lettings
	%	%
Before 1945	6	3
1945 to 1956	5	4
1957 to 1964	5	5
1965 to 1979	17	16
1980 to 1988	26	22
1989 to 1994	42	50
Total	**100**	**100**
(Base)	(253)	(454)

4.21 With this caveat in mind, Table 4.11 shows the date of first letting of the properties by the present landlord, excluding the don't knows. The differences between the two samples are not statistically significant. Hardly any of the lettings in both samples were first made before the second world war. In fact, in both samples roughly seven out of 10 were first made in 1980 or later. Forty-two % of all lettings and 50% of most recent lettings were made after rents were deregulated in January 1989.

4.22 Once again there were significant differences between the three landlord types. In both samples, lettings owned by sideline landlords were first let much more recently than was the case of lettings owned by business and institutional landlords. In the all lettings sample, 48% of lettings owned by sideline landlords had first been let after 1988, while 75% had first been let after 1979. In the most recent lettings sample, the figures were even larger: 57% and 80% respectively (Table 4.12).

Table 4.12 : Year landlord first let the accommodation by type of landlord						
	All lettings			Most recent lettings		
	Business	Sideline	Institution	Business	Sideline	Institution
	%	%	%	%	%	%
Before 1945	11	5	5	5	2	8
1945 to 1956	3	3	23	5	3	13
1957 to 1964	3	5	9	11	3	10
1965 to 1979	29	12	32	28	13	18
1980 to 1988	26	27	18	23	23	15
1989 to 1994	29	48	14	28	57	38
Total	**100**	**100**	**100**	**100**	**100**	**100**
(Base)	(38)	(193)	(22)	(75)	(337)	(40)

4.23 In both samples (but particularly the all lettings sample) lettings owned by institutions tended to be first let earlier than those owned by business and sideline landlords. In the all lettings sample, 37% of lettings owned by institutional landlords had first been let before 1965, compared with 17% owned by business landlords and 13 % owned by sideline landlords. In the most recent lettings sample, 31% owned by institutions had been first let before 1965, compared with 21% owned by business landlords and eight % owned by sideline landlords (Table 4.12).

4.24 Compared with their share of lettings, sideline landlords were over represented in both samples among properties that had been first let by the present owner after 1988 or later and under represented among those that had been first let before 1957. In the all lettings sample, institutional landlords were over represented among those which had first been let in the early post war years (1945 to 1956) - a period during which there was a significant deficit of housing to let and a relative shortage of labour - and to a lesser extent in the years from 1956 to 1979; they were under represented among properties that had first been let between 1980 and 1994. In the most recent lettings sample, institutional landlords were over represented among properties that had first been let prior to 1965; and slightly under represented among properties that were first let after 1979.

4.25 Business landlords showed a different pattern from the other two types of landlord in their relative share of the year in which lettings were first made. In the *all lettings sample*, business landlords were over represented among pre-war lettings. They were under represented among those let in the years from 1945 to 1964, a period when the privately rented sector was in steep decline. They were over represented among lettings first made between 1965 and 1979 and proportionately represented among lettings first made between 1980 and 1988, periods when the regulated tenancy system was in full operation. However, they were under represented among lettings first made after 1988, during which time new lettings were deregulated. In the *most recent lettings sample*, business landlords were over represented among properties that had been first let by the present owner in all periods up to 1979. In the period from 1980 to 1988 business landlords were proportionately represented and in the period since 1988 under represented.

4.26 Sideline landlords were over represented, and business landlords under represented, among properties which were first let after the 1988 Housing Act. This lends support to the finding that much of the increase in private lettings since 1988 has been due to the property slump and not just to investors responding to the changes made by the 1988 Act (Crook *et al.*, 1995). This issue is explored further in Chapter 5 and in Chapter 13.

Reasons for first letting the accommodation

4.27 Landlords in both samples gave a wide range of reasons as to why they had first started letting the accommodation. The landlords of 12% of all lettings and the landlords of 13% of most recent lettings said they had first let the accommodation in order to help pay the mortgage (or in a very few cases, their rent). Nine % and 12% respectively said they had first let the accommodation to help pay the running costs. The landlords of 20% of all lettings and of 26% of most recent lettings said they had done so in order to provide an income. Twenty % and 23% respectively said they had originally let the accommodation in order to provide a return on the investment. Sixteen % and 10% said it had been to house an employee. Four % in both samples said it was to make use of the space, while eight % and seven % respectively said they had let the accommodation in order to help someone out.

4.28 A third of the all lettings sample, and half of the most recent lettings sample of landlords gave more than one reason for first letting the accommodation. Table 4.13 shows the only or the single most important reason why the owner had taken this course of action. The differences between the two samples were not statistically significant. Less than half in both samples had first been let either to obtain a return for investment purposes or to provide an income. The desire to house an employee or to help with the mortgage repayments were other common reasons why the landlord had originally started letting the accommodation. A minority of other non investment reasons lay behind the landlords' decision to start letting the accommodation.

Table 4.13 : Single most important reason for first letting the accommodation		
	All lettings	Most recent letting
	%	%
To help pay the mortgage/rent	12	13
To help pay running expenses	4	5
To provide an income	18	23
To provide a return on an investment	18	21
To provide accommodation for an employee	20	13
For companionship	1	-
To make use of space	2	3
To help someone out	8	7
Already let when acquired	7	6
Some other reason	11	9
Total	**100**	**100**
(Base)	(212)	(326)

4.29 There were again significant differences within each of the two samples. The pattern of these differences was broadly the same for each sample. By far the most important reason why lettings owned by institutional landlords were first let was to house an employee; this was especially true of those in the all lettings sample, among which 64% had been first let for this reason. In both samples, lettings owned by business landlords were much more likely than those owned by the others to have been first let in order to obtain an income or to get a return on an investment. Lettings owned by sideline landlords were more likely than the others to have been let originally in order to help with the mortgage or help with running expenses (Table 4.14).

Table 4.14 : Single most important reason for first letting the accommodation by type of landlord						
	All lettings			Most recent lettings		
	Business	Sideline	Institution	Business	Sideline	Institution
	%	%	%	%	%	%
To help pay the mortgage/rent	5	15	-	7	16	-
To help pay running expenses	-	5	-	2	6	5
To provide an income	35	16	-	39	21	8
To provide a return on an investment	33	16	5	37	19	8
To provide accommodation for an employee	8	17	64	2	11	46
For companionship	-	1	-	-	-	-
To make use of space	-	3	-	-	3	3
To help someone out	5	8	9	2	8	11
Already let when acquired	10	7	-	10	6	3
Some other reason	5	11	23	3	10	16
Total	**100**	**100**	**100**	**100**	**100**	**100**
(Base)	(40)	(150)	(22)	(62)	(227)	(37)

5   Attitudes to letting

Summary

- Nearly half of all privately rented addresses were regarded by their owners as an investment, either for rental income or for capital growth; among the sample of most recent lettings made by landlords, just over half were viewed in this way;

- 'Continuing landlords' were more likely than new ones to view the address as an investment or as somewhere to house an employee. 'New landlords' were more likely than continuing ones to view the address as somewhere to live or as their home which they were unable or unwilling to sell;

- Lettings made by business landlords were much more likely than those made by sideline and especially by institutional landlords to be viewed as an investment;

- Most landlords and agents held positive attitudes to what it is like to let accommodation privately nowadays;

- Business landlords were a little more likely to be positive in their outlook to letting accommodation than were sideline and institutional landlords;

- Having an income from rent and, to a lesser extent, capital gains were mentioned as good things about being a landlord by large proportions of landlords and agents, but matters that were not directly financial, like providing accommodation for others and helping the local community, were also mentioned as good things by a significant minority;

- Repairs, arrears, troublesome tenants, getting repossession and the time taken up looking after property were most often mentioned as the worst things about being a landlord.

Introduction

5.1   The Department of the Environment's recent qualitative research study of private landlords (Thomas and Snape, 1995) has shed new light on what motivates them, how they operate, and their experiences of letting accommodation (see also Bevan *et al.*, 1995). This chapter complements the qualitative research by presenting a quantitative analysis of private landlord's attitudes to letting in the early post deregulation era. In particular, it examines how landlords and their agents regarded the sampled address or their most recent letting; their attitudes towards a range of issues to do with letting accommodation; and what they thought were the best things, and the worst things, about being a landlord.

How landlords viewed the letting

5.2   There was a significant difference between how landlords regarded the sampled letting and how they regarded the most recent letting which they had made, though the differences were not very large (Table 5.1). This is not surprising because a greater percentage of most recent lettings than of all lettings had been made since rents were deregulated in January 1989.

5.3   Nearly half of the all lettings sample were regarded by the landlord mainly as an investment, either for rental income or for capital growth. Over half of the most recent lettings were regarded in the same way by the landlord. Compared with the all lettings sample, the most recent lettings were less likely to be regarded as an investment for capital growth and much more likely to be viewed as an investment for rental income. Since a greater proportion of the recent lettings than the all lettings sample (92% compared with 73%) comprised tenancies which began after 15 January 1989, this difference is likely to have reflected the fall in house prices which has occurred in the post rent deregulation era and landlords' expectations about future house prices and rents.

Table 5.1 : How landlords viewed the property today	All lettings	Most recent letting
	%	%
As an investment for capital growth	22	16
As an investment for rental income	26	39
To live in (at some time)	7	6
As my home which I am unable/unwilling to sell at present	3	6
To house an employee	15	11
To help someone out	5	7
Incidental to another transaction	3	4
As a liability	10	8
Something else	9	4
Don't know	1	*
Total	**100**	**100**
(Base)	(212)	(329)

Base: all addresses where the respondent was a landlord

5.4   Properties in the most recent lettings sample were twice as likely to be seen as the landlord's home which they were unable or unwilling to sell at present, though the proportions in both samples giving this answer were small.

The all lettings sample were also more likely than the recent lettings sample to be regarded as somewhere to house an employee.

5.5   More marked than the differences *between* the two samples was the differences *within* them between the three types of landlord which were identified in Chapter 3. These within sample differences were broadly the same in the two samples. In both samples, lettings owned by business landlords were much more likely than the others (especially the institutional landlords) to be viewed as an investment. In the all lettings sample, the owners of 83% of lettings held by business landlords viewed the sampled address in this way; in the most recent lettings sample, 90% viewed their most recent letting as an investment. Investment reasons were also the most commonly mentioned way in which sideline landlords viewed the sampled letting or the most recent letting, but to a much lesser extent than business landlords. Among sideline landlords, 44% of addresses in the all lettings sample and 52% in the recent lettings sample were regarded as investments. Among institutional landlords, by far the most common way in which the sampled letting or the most recent letting was viewed was as somewhere to house an employee (Table 5.2).

5.6   There were statistically significant differences between 'new' and 'continuing' landlords as to how they regarded the address. In both samples, continuing landlords were more likely than new ones to view the address as an investment or as somewhere to house an employee. New landlords were more likely than continuing ones to view the address as somewhere to live or as their home which they were unable or unwilling to sell. In the all lettings sample, 50% of addresses owned by continuing landlords were regarded as an investment compared with 44% of addresses owned by new landlords. In the recent lettings sample, the figures were 61% and 43% respectively. In the all lettings sample, 13% of addresses owned by continuing landlords compared with two % owned by new landlords, were regarded as somewhere to house an employee. In the recent lettings sample, the figures were 12% and three % respectively. In the all lettings sample, 17% of addresses owned by new landlords compared with five % owned by continuing landlords, were regarded as somewhere to live. In the recent lettings sample, the figures were three % and 15% respectively. In the all lettings sample, seven % of addresses owned by new landlords compared with two % owned by continuing landlords, were regarded as the owner's home which they were unable or unwilling to sell at present. In the recent lettings sample, the figures were four % and 11% respectively.

5.7   In the second round of interviews (the recent lettings sample) two additional questions were asked of agents that had not been included in the original questionnaire. These ascertained whether the owner of their most recent letting was unable or unwilling to sell the property until house prices rise, and whether the owner lived in the UK or abroad.

5.8   Twenty-two % of the lettings in the recent lettings sample where the agent was interviewed were owned by property slump landlords; these accounted for eight % of the recent lettings sample as a whole. Property slump landlords were thus more likely than landlords as a whole to use a managing agent. In total - adding together those where an agent was interviewed and those where it was

	All lettings			Most recent lettings		
Table 5.2 : How landlords viewed the property by type of landlord						
	Business	Sideline	Institution	Business	Sideline	Institution
	%	%	%	%	%	%
As an investment for capital growth	33	23	-	16	18	5
As an investment for rental income	50	21	9	74	34	16
To live in (at some time)	-	10	-	2	8	-
As my home which I am unable/unwilling to sell at present	-	4	-	2	7	-
To house an employee	3	12	59	2	7	49
To help someone out	10	3	9	2	8	11
Incidental to another transaction	-	4	-	-	5	5
As a liability	3	13	-	3	11	-
Something else	-	9	23	-	3	14
Don't know	3	1	-	-	*	-
Total	**100**	**100**	**100**	**100**	**100**	**100**
(Base)	(40)	(150)	(22)	(62)	(229)	(37)

Base: addresses where landlords were interviewed

the landlord - 11% of the entire recent lettings sample was owned by property slump landlords.

5.9   Twenty-seven % of lettings in the recent lettings sample where the agent was interviewed were owned by people currently living abroad rather than in the UK; these accounted for six % of lettings in the recent lettings sample as a whole. While it is not surprising that these absentee landlords make use of managing agents, the survey has revealed that they are a major source of business for managing agents.

Views on letting accommodation

5.10   Landlords and agents in both samples were presented with a series of statements about *what it is like to let accommodation nowadays* and asked whether they agreed or disagreed with each of them in turn. The results are presented in Table 5.3. The general picture that emerges is that most landlords and agents were positive rather than negative in their attitudes to what it is like to let accommodation privately nowadays. On balance, agents were a little more positive in their outlook than landlords. However, between one tenth and three tenths of respondents felt able neither to agree nor to disagree with the various statements.

5.11   Respondents at 58% of addresses where the landlord was interviewed and 69% where the agent was interviewed, agreed with the statement that *Landlords find that tenants generally look after accommodation*. Respondents at 70% of addresses where the landlord was interviewed and 72% where the agents was interviewed, agreed rather than disagreed with the statement that *Landlords find that tenants are generally good at paying the rent on time*. Respondents at 67% of addresses where the landlord was interviewed and at 86% of addresses where the agent was interviewed, agreed that *The law allows landlords to charge a reasonable level of rent these days* (Table 5.3).

5.12   Respondents at 66% of addresses where the landlord was interviewed and at 84% of addresses where the agent was interviewed, disagreed with the view that *Landlords only let if they can't sell*. Seventy-one % and 76% respectively disagreed with the statement that *Landlords find it difficult to fill their vacancies* (Table 5.3).

5.13   Opinions were more mixed on four of the statements (see Table 5.3). More landlords and many more agents agreed than disagreed with the view that *On new lettings, landlords are adequately protected by the law against tenants refusing to leave*. More landlords and agents agreed than disagreed with the statement that *Landlords are expected to provide accommodation of a very high standard*. More landlords and many more agents disagreed with the statement that *Landlords spend a lot of their time arranging new lets because tenants move so frequently*. Both landlords and agents were about equally as likely to disagree as to agree that *Landlords find that wear and tear on rented property is quite small*.

Table 5.3 : Attitudes to letting accommodation by type of respondent

	Landlords					Agents				
	Agree	Neither agree nor disagree	Dis-agree	Total	(Base)	Agree	Neither agree nor disagree	Dis-agree	Total	(Base)
	%	%	%	%		%	%	%	%	
Landlords find that tenants generally look after accommodation	58	22	21	100	(539)	69	18	13	100	(270)
Landlords are expected to provide accomm-odation of a very high standard	52	29	20	100	(539)	44	26	30	100	(270)
Landlords find that tenants are generally good at paying the rent on time	70	19	11	100	(537)	72	17	11	100	(270)
Landlords find that wear and tear on rented property is quite small	42	17	40	100	(539)	39	24	37	100	(270)
Landlords only let if they can't sell	16	17	66	100	(533)	6	9	84	100	(270)
The law allows a landlord to charge a reasonable level of rent these days	67	19	14	100	(537)	86	5	9	100	(269)
Landlords spend a lot of time arranging new lets because tenants move so frequently	33	22	45	100	(538)	22	12	66	100	(270)

Landlords find it difficult to fill their vacancies	11	18	71	100	(539)	9	16	76	100	(270)
On new lettings, landlords are adequately protected by the law against tenants refusing to leave	46	33	20	100	(539)	67	9	24	100	(270)

Base: all addresses

5.14 There were statistically significant differences in the responses (at the 99% confidence level) between the landlord types on three out of the nine statements (Table 5.4). Overall, business landlords were a little more likely to be positive in their outlook than were sideline and institutional landlords. First, landlords of eight out of ten lettings owned by business landlords, compared with only two thirds of those owned by sideline and institutional landlords, agreed with the view that *Landlords find that tenants are generally good at paying the rent on time*. Second, the landlords of three quarters of addresses owned by business landlords, compared with two thirds of those owned by sideline landlords and only two fifths of those owned by institutional landlords, disagreed with the statement that *Landlords only let if they can't sell*. And, third, the landlords of three quarters of lettings owned by business landlords, compared with two thirds of those owned by sideline landlords and just under half of those owned by institutional landlords, agreed that *The law allows landlords to charge a reasonable level of rent these days*.

5.15 There were no statistically significant differences in views on these nine statements between those landlords who had acquired some or all of their lettings since rents were deregulated in January 1989, and those that had not acquired any of them since that date. Taking both interview sweeps together, there were also no statistically significant differences on these statements between landlords that had acquired all of their current stock of lettings since 1989 ('new landlords') and those that had acquired all or some of them before that date ('continuing landlords').

5.16 When the two interview sweeps were analysed separately, however, there were some statistically significant differences (at the 99% confidence level) between new and continuing landlords in respect of two of the statements; for the other seven statements, there were no statistically significant differences. First, continuing landlords were much more likely to agree with the statement that *Landlords find that tenants are generally good at paying the rent on time* and much less likely to disagree with it than were new landlords. Among the all lettings sample, the owners of three quarters (74%) of lettings held by continuing landlords agreed with this statement and only about one in twenty (six %) disagreed with it; while just over half (54%) of the owners of lettings made by new landlords agreed and a quarter (24%) disagreed. About a fifth of both types of owner were unable to express a view one way or the other. These differences did not exist among the most recent lettings sample.

Table 5.4 : Attitudes to letting by type of landlord														
	Business					Sideline					Institutional				
	Agree	Neither agree nor dis-agree	Dis-agree	Total	(Base)	Agree	Neither agree nor dis-agree	Dis-agree	Total	(Base)	Agree	Neither agree nor dis-agree	Dis-agree	Total	(Base)
	%	%	%	%		%	%	%	%		%	%	%	%	
Landlords find that tenants generally look after accomm-odation	51	26	23	100	(103)	60	19	22	100	(378)	58	32	11	100	(57)
Landlords are expected to provide accomm-odation of a very high standard	53	22	24	100	(103)	49	32	20	100	(378)	70	19	11	100	(57)
Landlords find that tenants are generally good at paying the rent on time	80	13	7	100	(102)	67	19	14	100	(378)	68	29	4	100	(56)
Landlords find that wear and tear on rented property is quite small	35	18	47	100	(103)	46	16	38	100	(378)	32	26	42	100	(57)
Landlords only let if they can't sell	14	12	75	100	(102)	18	14	68	100	(374)	9	50	41	100	(56)
The law allows a landlord to charge a reason-able level of rent these days	73	13	15	100	(103)	68	17	15	100	(377)	46	46	7	100	(56)
Landlords spend a lot of time arranging new lets because tenants move so frequently	38	14	49	100	(103)	35	24	42	100	(377)	18	26	56	100	(57)

Landlords find it difficult to fill their vacancies	16	12	73	100	(103)	11	19	70	100	(378)	4	19	77	100	(57)
On new lettings, landlords are adequately protected by the law against tenants refusing to leave	50	25	25	100	(103)	47	34	19	100	(378)	40	40	19	100	(57)

Base: addresses where landlords were interviewed

5.17 Second, among the most recent lettings sample, new landlords were more likely to agree and less to disagree than continuing landlords with the statement that *Landlords only let if they can't sell*. Thus, the owners of a quarter (24%) of lettings made by new landlords agreed and three fifths (60%) disagreed with this statement; while the owners of a tenth (10%) of lettings made by continuing landlords agreed and three quarters (73%) disagreed with it. About one in six owners of both types were unable to express a view either way. This difference did not apply among the all lettings sample.

5.18 There were no statistically significant differences in opinions about these nine statements about what it is like to let accommodation nowadays, between landlords who had inherited the sampled address and those that had acquired it in some other way. This was true when the two interview sweeps were analysed together and separately. Inheritor landlords were as positive about letting accommodation privately as were non-inheritor landlords; they were not disenchanted or reluctant owners of housing to let. This statement does not necessarily apply to all people who inherit accommodation because many of those who did not want to be landlords would have sold the property that they had acquired in this way.

The best things about being a landlord

5.19 The landlords and agents whose properties were included in the second sweep of the survey were asked what were the best and worst things about being a landlord. Most mentioned only one (60%) or two (29%) matters as the best things. Similarly most mentioned only one (46 percent) or two (31 percent) issues as the worst things.

5.20 As far as the best things are concerned, landlords of one in five addresses said that there was 'nothing' that could be described as the 'best' thing. Only one in 20 addresses had agents however who said this (Table 4.5). There were no significant differences between different types and sizes of landlords saying that nothing could be described a the 'best' thing (Table 5.6). Only a small proportion (four %) of addresses had landlords and agents who thought that the question was irrelevant.

5.21 Four things that related to the economic and financial side of being a landlord were mentioned amongst the best things: getting capital growth, providing income from rents, providing a contribution to a mortgage, and being a good way of making a living.

5.22 One in five addresses had landlords who said that getting capital growth was one of the best things, and three in 10 addresses had agents who said this. Some landlords were more likely to say this than others. A quarter of the addresses owned by sideline landlords who regarded their most recent letting as an investment (28%) or by business landlords (24%) cited capital growth as one of the best things - more than other sideline landlords and institution landlords. However, neither large nor small landlords were more likely than others to say this (Table 5.6).

Table 5.5 : The 'best' things about being a landlord		
Best things	Percent of addresses whose landlords stated the view listed	Percent of addresses whose agents stated the view listed
Nothing	18	5
Irrelevant question	4	4
Having an investment for capital growth	19	30
Providing a rental income	33	57
Providing a contribution to a mortgage	4	4
A good way to earn a living	9	4
Providing a service to a local community	16	9
Security	7	18
Sociability/companionship	8	2
Independence/flexibility	2	3
Satisfaction of having good tenants	5	6
Providing accommodation for others	6	1
Others	1	10
Vague reply	1	2
Don't know	1	2
(Base)	(331)	(181)
Base: all addresses in the recent lettings sample		

5.23 Getting an income from rent was mentioned as the best thing by the landlords and agents of a much greater proportion of addresses than mentioned capital growth or anything else. It was mentioned by the landlords of a third of the addresses (33%) and by the agents of nearly six in 10 addresses (57%) (Table 5.5). It was mentioned more by business landlords and investment motivated sideline landlords than by others, although it was equally of importance to landlords of all sizes (Table 5.6).

5.24 Whilst only four % of addresses had landlords and agents who thought that getting a contribution to a mortgage was the best thing (Table 5.5), this was more important to sideline landlords who did not regard their most recent letting as an investment and to those with only one letting in total (Table 5.6). There were also significant differences in the extent to which different landlords thought the best thing was being able to make a good living. Nine % of addresses had landlords who thought this but only four % of addresses had agents who mentioned it (Table 5.5). Business landlords (30%) and larger landlords mentioned this more often than others (Table 56). It was noteworthy that landlords who identified this as the best thing were more likely than others to have asked tenants to leave accommodation at least once since 1988 and to have taken court action than landlords who did not mention this as the best thing. For example 72% had asked someone to leave, compared with 44% of others.

Table 5.6 : The 'best' things about being a landlord by type and size of landlord

Best things	Proportion of addresses							
	Type of landlord				Size of lettings portfolio			
	Sideline		Business	Institution	1	2-7	8-40	41+
	Not an investment	An investment						
Nothing	23	15	16	4	21	22	17	11
Irrelevant question	6	2	3	5	7	1	3	4
Having an investment for capital growth	11	28	24	-	13	25	23	17
Providing a rental income	23	50	29	9	29	39	36	28
Providing a contribution to a mortgage	9	1	2	-	10	5	-	-
A good way to earn a living	-	8	30	-	1	5	8	12
Providing a service to a local community	17	16	11	27	12	12	14	27
Security	10	6	-	9	14	2	4	5
Sociability/ companionship	9	7	13	-	10	7	10	6

Independence/ flexibility	-	1	11	-	-	1	3	6
Satisfaction of having good tenants	2	8	3	5	8	3	5	4
Providing accomm-odation for others	11	1	-	23	-	5	6	12
Other	1	2	-	4	1	-	3	1
Vague reply	-	2	2	4	1	-	1	2
Don't know	-	1	-	4	1	1	-	-
(Base)	(123)	(123)	(63)	(22)	(91)	(81)	(78)	(81)

5.25 All the other best things listed in Table 5.5 cover a wide range of matters, although none of them are, at least directly, financial in character. Some are about providing accommodation for others (six % of addresses had landlords who said this) or about providing a service to the community (16%) (Table 5.5). Being able to provide accommodation for others was mentioned mainly by sideline landlords who did not regard their most recent letting as an investment and by institution landlords and more by larger than smaller landlords (Table 5.6).

5.26 The other things noted which were essentially non financial in character were related to gaining security through being a landlord (especially by smaller landlords), having independence and flexibility (especially larger and business landlords), the sociability and companionship of landlordship (mentioned by almost all types and sizes of landlords) and the satisfaction of having good tenants (Tables 5.5 and 5.6).

The worst things about being a landlord

5.27 The 'worst' things about being a landlord mentioned by landlords are listed in Table 5.7 and fall into two groups: financial or economic and management problems (although these, too, have financial implications).

5.28 Respondents at only nine % of addresses where the landlord was interviewed and one % where the agent was interviewed could not identify anything that was the 'worst' thing about being a landlord (Tables 5.7 and 5.8).

5.29 The cost of repairs, dealing with rent arrears, Housing Benefit problems, low rents and returns, continuing rent control and paying tax on rents were the six worst things mentioned that were financial in nature. Of these, repairs and arrears were mentioned far more than the others. Nineteen % and 16% of addresses had landlords who mentioned repairs and arrears respectively. Twenty-eight % and 43% of agents mentioned repairs and arrears (Table 5.7). These two things were identified by all types and sizes of landlords. Those landlords who had asked a tenant to leave at least once since 1988 were significantly more likely to mention arrears (21%) than those who had not asked a tenant to leave (12%). It is noteworthy that respondents at only four % of addresses where the landlord was interviewed and five % where it was the agent, mentioned low rents or returns amongst the worst things identified (Table 5.7).

5.30 Amongst the many matters related to looking after property, having troublesome tenants stands out as being the worst thing about being a landlord and was mentioned by more landlords and agents than any other. Over a third of addresses (35%) had landlords who said this and over half (56%) have agents who stated it (Table 5.7). It was of lesser importance only to institutional landlords (many of who house employees), but otherwise was mentioned in similar proportions by all types and sizes of landlords (Table 5.8). Those mentioning it were much more likely to have asked a tenant to leave at least once since 1988 (46%) than those who did not (29%).

Table 5.7 : The 'worst' things about being a landlord		
Worst things	Percent of addresses whose landlords stated the view listed	Percent of addresses whose agents stated the view listed
Nothing	9	1
Irrelevant question	1	3
Cost of repairs	19	28
Arrears	16	43
Housing Benefit	5	3
Low rents/returns	4	5
Continued rent control	1	1
Tax on rental income	2	7
Difficulty getting grants	1	1
Worries about voids	1	7
Troublesome tenants	35	56
Getting repossession	8	15
Not enough protection from the law	4	4
Too much legislative change	1	3
Problems getting agreements drawn up	2	3
Time taken dealing with management	20	11
Worries about keeping eye on things	2	1
Bad image	5	4
Don't want to be a landlord	1	2

Others	7	14
Vague answers	2	1
Don't know	1	1
(Base)	(331)	(181)

Base: all landlords and agents in second survey sweep

5.31 The other worst things mentioned by more than a handful of respondents were getting repossession (eight % of landlords and 15% of agents) and the time taken up with dealing with matters (20% of landlords and 11% of agents) (Table 5.7). These were mentioned in approximately equal proportions by all types of landlords but by rather more larger than smaller landlords (Table 5.8).

5.32 The fact that some issues were identified by so few landlords and agents is noteworthy. For example, comparatively few mentioned voids, not having enough protection through the law, and that landlords had a bad image (Table 5.7). However, it should be noted that business, investment motivated sideline landlords and larger landlords mentioned the bad image more often than others (Table 5.8).

Table 5.8 : The worst things about being a landlord by type and size of landlord

Best things	Proportion of addresses							
	Type of landlord				Size of lettings portfolio			
	Sideline		Business	Institution	1	2-7	8-40	41+
	Not an invest-ment	An invest-ment						
Nothing	14	7	5	9	14	11	6	5
Irrelevant question	1	1	-	-	2	-	-	-
Cost of repairs	21	23	9	14	20	21	24	11
Arrears	15	18	17	14	16	15	15	18
Housing Benefit	2	6	9	-	-	4	11	5
Low rents/returns	5	5	3	4	3	7	4	4
Continued rent control	2	1	2	-	-	4	1	-
Tax on rental income	2	3	3	-	2	2	4	1
Difficulty getting grants	2	2	-	-	-	1	3	1
Worries about voids	2	-	-	-	1	1	-	-
Troublesome tenants	33	37	51	14	36	44	33	32

Getting possession	5	11	9	9	8	2	15	7
Not enough protection from the law	3	5	5	-	1	5	3	7
Too much legislative change	2	1	2	-	-	-	1	4
Problems getting agreements drawn up	4	2	-	-	2	1	4	1
Time taken dealing with matters	18	22	22	18	11	20	22	30
Worries about keeping eye on things	2	4	-	-	4	4	-	-
Bad image	-	5	17	-	1	2	6	11
Don't want to be a landlord	-	2	-	-	2	-	-	-
Others	9	6	2	14	4	5	6	11
(Base)	(123)	(123)	(63)	(22)	(91)	(81)	(78)	(81)

Base: the recent lettings sample of addresses where the landlords was interviewed

53

6   Tenancy arrangements

Summary

6.1   The key findings of this chapter are:

- assured shorthold tenancies were used for most lettings made since deregulation;

- a large minority of lettings had landlords who did not know what tenancy agreement they were using;

- informal networks were an important means of finding tenants, especially where the landlords, rather than agents, managed lettings;

- most lettings were preceded by only a short void period;

- rents for only a small proportion of new lettings were negotiated;

- deposits and/or rent in advance were paid by the tenants of most lettings made since deregulation.

Introduction

6.2   When letting accommodation, landlords are faced with a number of decisions, including the type of tenancy agreement to use, what rent to charge (and whether to fix it at the outset or to be willing to negotiate with prospective tenants), and whether to ask for a deposit and/or rent in advance and, if so, how much. Landlords also need to decide how to advertise vacancies or what other means to use in order to find new tenants.

6.3   The next chapter looks at the rents charged for these lettings - and the returns obtained by the landlords. Chapter 9 examines landlords' general attitudes towards the legal framework for letting.

6.4   This chapter looks at two aspects of the tenancy arrangements for lettings in the two samples:

- the **types of letting agreement** used;

- key aspects of the **letting process**, including void periods prior to letting, advertising methods, rent negotiation and deposits.

Letting accommodation: types of agreement used

6.5   There were important differences in the agreements landlords had with the tenants in the two surveys, because of the different way the samples were drawn. Because the 'all lettings' sample is based on a representative sample of all private rented addresses in England, it includes a number where the most recent letting at those addresses dates back many years (see Chapter 4), including 37% where the most recent letting was prior to the rent deregulation that took place in January 1989. In contrast, because the 'recent lettings' sample is based on the most recent letting (wherever located) made by the landlords of a representative sample of all private rented addresses, a greater proportion of these have been let more recently, including 91% since deregulation and, hence, are 1988 Housing Act lettings (Table 6.1).

Table 6.1: Types of letting agreement with most recent tenant						
Type of agreement	All lettings managed by			Recent lettings managed by		
	Landlord	Agent	All	Landlord	Agent	All
	%	%	%	%	%	%
Assured tenancy	5	9	6	7	7	7
Assured shorthold tenancy	24	58	34	57	82	66
Shorthold (80 Act) tenancy	5	-	4	4	1	3
Regulated (Rent Act) tenancy	17	20	18	4	1	3
Nonexclusive occupancy licence	<1	-	<1	1	-	<1
Holiday let (off season)	-	-	-	-	1	<1
Holiday let (in season)	-	-	-	<1	-	<1
Company let	1	-	1	-	2	1
Accommodation tied to job	12	7	11	6	1	4
Accommodation with meals and laundry	1	-	1	<1	-	<1
Something else	27	4	20	15	4	11
Don't know	7	1	5	6	1	3
Base	212	89	301	331	181	512
Base: all lettings						

6.6   Some of the key characteristics of **all lettings** were as follows:

- five % of the addresses were wholly vacant and six % of the most recent lettings were vacant at the time of the survey;

- thirty-eight % were let furnished, including partly furnished;

- seven % were let to a relative of the landlord;

- seventeen % went with a job, and at 80% of these addresses the tenants would be legally obliged to leave the accommodation if they gave up their jobs;

- sixty-six % were lettings where the tenant had signed a written agreement;

6.7   The key characteristics of **recent lettings** were similar, with some differences. Thus:

- five % of the addresses were wholly vacant and six % of the most recent lettings were vacant;

- fifty-two % were furnished, more than for all lettings;

- six % were let to the landlords' relatives;

- eight % went with the tenants' jobs (at 82% of addresses the tenants would have to leave if they left the job);

- at 86% of the lettings, the tenants had a written agreement (because of the bigger proportion of assured shorthold tenancies amongst recent lettings).

6.8   When landlords were asked to describe the type of letting agreement which they had used, the landlords and agents of a quarter of the all lettings sample either did not know (five %) or described a type of letting that was not legally recognized (20%) (Table 6.1). Although rather smaller proportions of recent lettings had landlords or agents who did not know (three %) or did not describe a legally recognized type (11%), these findings suggest that many lettings had landlords who were not well informed about the legal framework for letting accommodation. In fact, as Table 6.1 also shows, this uncertainty was largely confined to landlords rather than to agents. For example, a third of all lettings and a fifth of recent lettings had landlords who either did not know the legal agreement they had with their tenant or described one that did not exist in law, compared with only five % of the agents managing both all lettings and recent lettings (Table 6.1).

6.9   As Table 6.1 also shows, 40% of all lettings were described as either assured tenancy agreements or assured shortholds, compared with over 73% of the most recent lettings (Table 6.1). Assured tenancy agreements covered only a small proportion of lettings. Assured shortholds covered 34% of all lettings and 66% of recent lettings (including over 82% of the most recent lettings managed by agents).

6.10   One of the conditions of an assured shorthold tenancy is that there must be a written agreement confirming that a shorthold has been created. It should be noted therefore that 96% and 99% respectively of assured shorthold agreements amongst all lettings and recent lettings were ones where the landlords and agents said there were written agreements.

6.11   Only four % of all lettings (and three % of recent lettings) were covered by shortholds created under the 1980 Housing Act - and over eight in 10 of these had written agreements. However, a further measure of landlords' uncertainty about of the legal framework for letting is that 80% of these were let after the 1988 Housing Act had come into operation in January 1989, replacing 1980 Act shortholds with the new assured shortholds.

6.12 As 90% recent lettings had been created since deregulation, the finding that only a small proportion (3%) of them were regulated (Rent Act) tenancies, is not unexpected. Again, it was to be expected that a much larger number of all lettings, 18%, would be covered by this type of agreement. Indeed, 46% of all lettings made before deregulation as well as 25% of recent lettings made before then were regulated tenancies (it is noteworthy that the landlords and agents of only 1% of lettings made after deregulation claimed these were covered by regulated tenancies). Furthermore at over 8 in 10 of regulated tenancies, the rent was a registered Fair Rent (85% of regulated tenancies amongst all lettings and 91% of those amongst recent lettings).

6.13 Apart from accommodation tied to a job, the remainder of the letting agreements identified covered only very small proportions of all lettings and of recent lettings. Tied accommodation accounted for 11% of all lettings and four % of recent lettings. It also covered a greater proportion of lettings managed by landlords than those managed by agents. For example 12% of all lettings managed by their owners were covered by tied accommodation agreements, compared with only seven % of all lettings managed by agents.

6.14 There were some distinctive differences in the types of agreement different sorts of landlords (who were managing accommodation themselves) had with their tenants, both with respect to their motivation (Table 6.2) and to the size of their portfolio of lettings (Table 6.3).

Table 6.2 : Types of letting agreement by type of landlords										
	All lettings					Recent lettings				
	Sideline landlords sample letting		Busi-ness	Instit-ution	All	Sideline landlords sample letting		Busi-ness	Instit-ution	All
	Non-invest-ment	Invest-ment				Non-invest-ment	Invest-ment			
	%	%	%	%	%	%	%	%	%	%
Assured tenancy	8	11	5	-	5	3	3	6	30	7
Assured shorthold tenancy	20	35	25	7	24	50	66	73	22	57
Shorthold (80 Act) tenancy	3	11	2	-	5	3	7	3	-	4
Regulated (Rent All) tenancy	9	18	40	-	17	3	6	-	3	4
Non exclusive occupancy licence	-	-	-	4	<1	-	2	-	-	1

Holiday let (off season)	-	-	-	-	-	-	-	-	-	-
Holiday let (in season)	-	-	-	-	-	-	1	-	-	<1
Company let	1	1	-	4	1	-	-	-	-	1
Accommodation tied to job	15	1	7	41	12	8	-	-	30	6
Accommodation with meals and laundry	1	-	2	-	1	1	-	-	<1	<1
Something else	32	23	17	36	27	23	8	14	16	15
Don't know	8	9	-	9	7	7	8	4	-	6
Base	84	66	40	22	212	113	118	63	37	331

Base: all lettings whose landlords were interviewed

6.15 A greater proportion of all lettings owned by sideline (especially those not regarded as investments) and by institutional landlords than by business landlords had owners who did not know what the tenancy agreement was (or identified something not recognised in law). Similarly a greater proportion of recent lettings owned by sideline landlords and not regarded as investments, were ones where the landlords did not know the tenancy agreement.

6.16 Nonetheless it is important to stress, that as many as 32% of all lettings owned by sideline landlords for investment purposes and 17% of all lettings owned by business landlords had owners who did not know what tenancy agreement they had or thought it was of a type that was not, in fact, recognized by law.

6.17 The other key differences in terms of landlord types (Table 6.2) are:

- Lettings owned by sideline landlords for investment purposes or by business landlords were more likely than others to be regulated tenancies;

- Lettings owned by sideline landlords for investments and by business landlords were also more likely than others to be assured or assured shorthold tenancies;

- Lettings owned by sideline landlords for noninvestment purposes and by institutions were more likely than others to be tied accommodation;

6.18 Size of portfolio is connected both with knowledge about letting agreements and with the type used, especially the degree to which lettings go with jobs of the tenants (Table 6.3).

Table 6.3 : Types of letting agreement by size of landlord's total lettings portfolio										
	All lettings					Recent lettings				
	1	2-8	9-40	41+	All	1	2-8	9-40	41+	All
	%	%	%	%	%	%	%	%	%	%
Assured tenancy	6	-	11	3	5	2	2	3	21	7
Assured shorthold tenancy	34	23	20	20	24	47	62	72	48	57
Shorthold (80 Act) tenancy	6	8	7	1	5	5	6	1	4	4
Regulated (Rent All) tenancy	6	18	24	19	17	4	6	3	1	4
Nonexclusive occupancy licence	-	-	-	1	<1	-	1	1	-	1
Holiday let (off season)	-	-	-	-	-	-	-	-	-	-
Holiday let (in season)	-	-	-	-	-	1	-	-	-	<1
Company let	2	-	-	3	1	-	-	-	-	-
Accommodation tied to job	-	3	4	32	12	1	4	9	11	6
Accommodation with meals and laundry	-	-	4	-	1	1	-	-	-	<1
Something else	38	25	27	20	27	21	14	10	12	5
Don't know	6	22	2	-	7	15	3	1	2	6
Base	47	51	45	69	212	91	81	78	81	331

Base: all lettings whose landlords were interviewed.

6.19 Small portfolio landlords were more likely to lack knowledge than ones with larger portfolios. For example 44% of all lettings (and 45% of recent lettings) which were the sole letting of their landlord had owners who did not know what agreement they had with their tenant or thought it was something that the law did not recognize. This compares with 20% of all lettings and 12% of recent lettings whose landlords owned 41 lettings or more in all (Table 6.3).

6.20 Tied accommodation was much more likely to be owned by larger than by smaller portfolio landlords. Thus none of the lettings owned by single letting landlords was covered by a tied accommodation agreement, compared with 32% of all lettings owned by landlords with more than 40 lettings in total (Table 6.3).

6.21 Only three % of all the lettings and four % of recent lettings had resident landlords. In 44% of all, and 40% of recent lettings, the landlord did not know what type of letting agreement covered the tenancies. The landlords of a third of all resident landlord lettings and a quarter of all recent resident landlord lettings said that the agreement covering the letting was an assured shorthold.

6.22 Assured shorthold agreements covered six in 10 of the lettings at addresses which were the previous homes of owner occupiers who had been unable to sell. All the rest of these were ones where the landlords did not know what the agreement was (in all cases where the agent handled the letting, the agreement was known - and was an assured shorthold). In cases where the landlord was abroad, 84% were let on assured shortholds.

Letting accommodation: finding tenants

6.23 As Table 6.4 shows, a large number of methods of finding tenants for the most recent lettings were employed. However, most landlords used only one technique. For example, where the landlords did the job themselves, tenants for the recent letting amongst the sample of all lettings were found using only one of the methods listed on Table 6.4. In contrast, where agents handled the letting, only 55% were filled using only one method of finding tenants.

Table 6.4 : Methods of finding tenants for most recent lettings						
	All lettings managed by			Recent lettings managed by		
	Landlord	Agent	All	Landlord	Agent	All
	%	%	%	%	%	%
Direct approach from prespective tenant	24	16	22	23	28	25
Placed ads in newspapers	11	37	19	22	41	29
Tenants already resident	15	1	11	6	1	4
Through relatives/friends of landlord	11	2	9	13	2	9
Through letting/estate agent	8	43	18	17	48	28
Through previous tenant	7	7	7	10	4	8
Colleagues at work/employers	5	1	4	5	3	4
Univ/College accommodation office/noticeboards	4	3	4	4	6	5
Placed ads in newsagent	3	5	4	3	3	3
Answer ads in newspapers	2	3	2	3	7	4
Tied accommodation	2	-	2	4	1	3
Referred from social services	1	1	1	2	4	4
Letting board at address	<1	2	1	-	-	-
Answer ads in newsagent	-	1	<1	<1	<1	<1
Other	15	19	16	8	7	7

Don't know	4	7	5	<1	<1	<1
Not applicable	-	6	3	<1	<1	<1
Base	212	89	301	331	181	512

Base: all lettings

6.24 Looking at the methods listed in more detail, it should be noted that many of them are based on using personal contacts, rather than more formal marketplace techniques, like advertising, although there was an important difference between the types of approaches used by landlords and by agents. It should also be noted that at 11% of lettings (15% of those where the letting was done by the landlord) the tenant was already resident at the time the letting was made, presumably taking over the tenancy from a friend or relative.

6.25 The significance of informal methods is emphasized by the facts that tenants were found for 22% of all lettings after direct approaches from prospective tenants, seven % through the previous tenant, nine % through relatives or friends of the landlord and four % through colleagues or employees at work (Table 6.4). It will be noted from Table 6.4 that reliance upon friends, relatives and workplace contacts was more important for landlords than for agents, but that direct approaches from prospective and previous tenants were methods used almost as much by agents as by landlords,

6.26 The comparative significance of more formal methods to agents is shown by the fact that 43% of all lettings made by them were as a result of finding the tenants themselves, but that 37% were also made following the placing of advertisements in newspapers. Only eight % and 11% of the lettings made by landlords used these two methods.

6.27 The other methods listed, such as placing advertisements on newsagents windows and using student accommodation offices, were used for a comparatively small proportion of lettings.

6.28 It should also be noted that the pattern of methods for finding tenants for the sample of recent lettings is broadly the same as for the sample of all lettings.

Table 6.5 : Methods landlords used for finding tenants for most recent lettings by type of landlord

	All lettings					Recent lettings				
	Sideline landlords sample letting		Busi-ness	Instit-ution	All	Sideline landlords sample letting		Busi-ness	Instit-ution	All
	Non-invest-ment	Invest-ment				Non-invest-ment	Invest-ment			
	%	%	%	%	%	%	%	%	%	%
Direct approach from prespective tenant	22	33	26	19	26	22	24	25	27	24
Placed ads in newspapers	5	21	13	-	11	18	28	36	6	28
Tenants already resident	12	15	30	-	15	5	8	7	3	7
Through relatives/friends of landlord	20	10	3	5	12	17	16	11	0	14
Through letting/estate agent	4	3	5	5	8	10	9	12	9	10
Through previous tenant	5	9	13	5	8	5	12	25	-	11
Colleagues at work/employers	11	-	3	5	5	10	4	2	3	5
Univ/College accommodation office/noticeboards	5	5	-	9	5	2	9	2	-	4
Placed ads in newsagent	5	3	3	-	4	1	5	5	-	3
Answer ads in newspapers	-	2	8	-	2	2	4	4	-	3
Tied accommodation	1	2	-	14	3	6	-	-	24	5
Referred from social services	1	-	-	-	<1	3	-	2	9	2
Letting board at address	-	-	-	-	-	-	-	-	-	-
Answer ads in newsagent	-	-	-	-	-	-	1	2	-	1
Other	18	7	10	43	16	10	3	7	27	9
Don't know	1	2	10	-	3	1	-	-	-	<1
Not applicable	-	-	-	-	-	-	1	-	-	<1
Base	74	57	39	21	191	92	105	56	-33	286

Base: all lettings managed by landlords excluding those let rent free.

6.29 There are, however, significant differences in the methods used by different types of landlords, where they make the lettings themselves (Table 6.5). Sideline landlords, who regarded their letting as an investment, and business landlords, relied more than others on formal than on informal methods.

Sideline landlords who did not regard their letting as an investment relied more than others on workplace colleagues and friends or relatives. Institutional landlords used other methods (not listed) more than others, but also their own employees (for tied accommodation) and referrals from social services (in the case of the sample of most recent lettings). Business landlords more than others made new lettings to those already in residence. Despite these differences, it needs to be stressed that all types of landlords used formal as well as informal methods, so that, for example, all of them received direct approaches from prospective tenants.

6.30 Not unexpectedly, the size of landlords' total lettings is also a factor related to the methods they used when finding tenants themselves (Table 6.6). In particular, small landlords made more use of friends and relatives than did other landlords.

Table 6.6 : Methods of finding tenants for most recent letting by size of landlords total lettings portfolio								
	All lettings				Recent lettings			
	1	2-8	9-40	41+	1	2-8	9-40	41+
	%	%	%	%	%	%	%	%
Direct approach from prespective tenant	21	20	35	26	16	21	26	33
Placed ads in newspapers	9	14	2	15	16	37	27	16
Tenants already resident	19	20	122	6	17	3	1	4
Through relatives/friends of landlord	31	14	7	1	22	15	13	4
Through letting/estate agent	7	4	2	3	14	6	9	10
Through previous tenant	5	7	5	12	9	10	14	11
Colleagues at work/employers	2	2	8	8	4	3	1	12
Univ/College accommodation office/noticeboards	9	7	-	3	3	9	6	-
Placed ads in newsagent	5	4	5	1	3	4	4	1
Answer ads in newspapers	-	2	5	1	4	1	6	-
Tied accommodation	-	4	-	5	-	3	10	7
Referred from social services	-	-	2	-	1	-	3	5
Letting board at address	-	-	-	-	-	-	-	-
Answer ads in newsagent	-	-	-	-	1	1	-	-
Other	5	9	15	28	4	2	9	21
Don't know	1	2	-	8	-	-	-	-

Not applicable	-	-	-	-	-	-	-	-
Base	42	44	40	65	77	67	69	73

Base: all lettings managed by landlords.

Letting accommodation: vacancy lengths

6.31 Landlords and agents were asked how long the most recent letting (if it had been made since deregulation) had been vacant before the tenant moved in. The question did not apply to all the lettings, as Table 6.7 shows, because in 19% cases the tenant was already living there (i.e. taking over from an existing tenant).

Table 6.7 : Length of vacancy between previous and most recent letting agreement for lettings made since 1989

	All lettings				Recent lettings			
	Assured and assured shorthold	All other types	Other and don't know	All	Assured and assured shorthold	All other types	Other and don't know	All
	%	%	%	%	%	%	%	%
<1 week	27	36	32	30	25	41	42	28
1 week <2	7	8	7	7	9	14	11	10
2 weeks <1 month	11	-	11	9	18	7	4	15
1 month < 3 months	20	22	7	18	23	20	16	22
3 months < 6 months	9	8	9	9	9	7	14	9
6 months < 12 months	3	3	2	3	4	-	2	4
12 months +	-	-	7	1	4	4	4	4
Don't know	4	3	7	4	3	2	5	3
Not applicable	18	19	18	19	5	4	2	5
Base:	108	36	44	188	369	44	55	468

Base: all lettings made since deregulation.

6.32 Thirty % of all lettings (and 28% of the most recent lettings) had been made within a week of the vacancy arising and only 13% of all lettings (15% of the most recent lettings) had been vacant for three months or more before the last tenant moved in.

6.33 There were significant differences between lettings in terms of the types of letting agreement that were used for the letting. In particular, assured and assured shorthold tenancies were preceded by longer void period than others.

For example only 34% of the most recent lettings made on assured or assured shorthold tenancies were made within two weeks, compared with 54% of those let on other types of agreement. This suggests that lettings which are not restricted in some way (like tied accommodation) and are fully available to the general public may be harder to let - or it may be that landlords needed to carry out repairs or decorations to these more than to others before finding a new tenant.

6.34 There were no significant differences in terms of the region where the letting was made, so that, for example, lettings did not follow longer voids period in the northern regions of England, than in the South East or other regions of England. Nor were there differences in terms of the year in which the letting was made, nor in the type and size of landlord. Thus, for example, larger landlords did not have shorter or longer voids periods prior to making lettings than others. Similarly, business oriented landlords had voids periods which were the same as other types of landlords. However, where landlords themselves were making the letting, they did so within a week in 32% of cases compared with only 23% of cases where agents were making the letting, suggesting that agents were not more likely to be able to fill vacancies faster than landlords themselves, all other things being equal.

Letting accommodation: negotiating the rent

6.35 As Table 6.8 shows, landlords and agents of only a small proportion of lettings made after deregulation negotiated the rent with the tenant. In over half the cases (57%) of all lettings made after deregulation, the rent was definitely fixed and not negotiable. This was also the case for 71% of the sample of most recent lettings. The fact that a greater proportion of all lettings than of recent lettings had landlords or agents where this was not applicable is due to the proportion of all lettings where tenants were already in residence and had taken over from the previous tenant.

Table 6.8 : Negotiation with tenant about rent for most recent lettings (made after deregulation) by type of letting agreement								
(a) negotiation	All lettings				Recent lettings			
	Assured and assured shorthold	All other types	Other and don't know	All	Assured and assured shorthold	All other types	Other and don't know	All
	%	%	%	%	%	%	%	%
Negotiated	29	3	18	21	23	18	33	23
Fixed	53	69	57	57	72	68	64	71
Don't know and not applicable	18	28	25	22	5	14	4	6
Base	108	36	44	188	369	44	55	468

Base: all lettings made after deregulation.

6.36 The extent to which landlords and agents negotiated rents was unrelated to the location (region) of the letting, and to the size and type of the landlord.

6.37 In very few cases (seven %) where rents were negotiated, did the negotiation result in a higher rent than the landlord or agent had originally intended to charge. In 60% of all lettings and in 39% of the most recent lettings, the outcome was a lower rent.

Letting accommodation : deposits and rent in advance

6.38 A large proportion of tenants paid deposits and/or rent in advance. Half the tenants of all lettings made since January 1989 did so, whilst three quarter of tenants of the most recent lettings paid one or more of these (Table 6.9). Looking only at lettings made since deregulation in January 1989, 63% of tenants paid deposits and/or rent in advance at the beginning of their tenancies, including 86% of those moving into lettings made on assured or assured shorthold tenancies.

Table 6.9 : Deposits and rent in advance paid by tenant of most recent lettings

	All lettings	Most recent letting
	%	%
Deposit	8	14
Rent in advance	16	15
Both	25	47
Neither	43	22
Don't know	8	2
Base	301	512

Base: all lettings.

6.39 Significant sums of money were involved (Table 6.10). The average deposit paid for all lettings commencing in either 1993 or 1994 was £644, equivalent to an average of 11% of the rent per annum charged at the time of the surveys (excluding lettings where rent was not charged). Where tenants paid rent in advance, they paid, on average, a similar sum (£626), or nine % of the annual rent. Where tenants paid both, the average payment involved was £1,048, or 22% of the annual rent.

Table 6.10 : Size of deposits and rent[£] in advance paid by tenant of most recent lettings (made in 1993 and 1994)

	All lettings			Most recent lettings		
	Average	Standard deviation	Base	Average	Standard deviation	Base
Deposit	385	254	48	452	634	278
Deposit as % annual rent	8	3	47	8	4	276
Rent in advance	626	1,250	51	534	937	280
Advance rent as % annual rent	9	5	50	9	9	280
Both (where paid)	813	449	41	1077	1512	223
Both as % annual rent	16	5	40	17	11	223

Base: all lettings made in 1993 and 1994.

7   Financial aspects of letting accommodation

Summary

- A minority of landlords did not charge rent for the accommodation at the address;

- Most landlords who did charge rent expected it to cover their costs, but only a substantial minority expected it to provide them with an investment return;

- The rent being charged on the most recent tenancy was considered to be sufficient by half of the landlords or agents in the all lettings sample and seven out of ten in the recent lettings sample;

- The average rent being charged at addresses where the rent was considered to be sufficient was much higher than where it was thought to be insufficient;

- Excluding rent-free addresses, rent was uncollected at 13% of addresses in the all lettings sample and 15% in the recent lettings sample; when averaged across all addresses where rent was charged, arrears accounted for about two % of the rent due;

- Excluding rent-free addresses, rent was lost due to vacancies at 17% of addresses in the all lettings sample and 45% in the recent lettings sample; averaged across all lettings where rent was charged, rent lost due to voids accounted for about two % of the rent due in the all lettings sample and six % in the recent lettings sample;

- Management and maintenance expenditure accounted for 30% of the rent in the all lettings sample and 26% in the recent lettings sample;

- Just over half of all addresses in both samples had had major repair or improvement work done to them since 1980; in a significant minority of cases, this work had been completed with the aid of a grant from the local authority;

- The average gross rental yield was 6.3% in the all lettings sample and 8.4% in the recent lettings sample; there was a considerable variation in yields around these averages;

- Average gross yields were about twice as high at addresses where the most recent tenancy had commenced after rent deregulation than on those which had commenced before then;

- Where landlords and agents thought that the rent from the letting was insufficient, the average difference between the gross rental yield on the address and that implied by the rent they felt would be sufficient, was about 3.6% in the all lettings sample and 4.1% in the recent lettings sample;

- Among addresses that had been purchased, the average annual change in the value of the address - comparing purchase price (adjusted for inflation) with estimated vacant possession value - was 5.4%;

- At one in eight of addresses landlords had said that they did not want a return from their portfolio of lettings; among those that did, there was an even split between addresses where the landlord thought the rental income was sufficient to cover all repairs and give a reasonable return and those that thought it was not sufficient.

Introduction

7.1 This chapter looks at some of the financial aspects of letting private accommodation. It examines rents and rent setting; what the rent was expected to cover and whether the rent was felt to be sufficient to cover these items; rent arrears and vacancies; management and maintenance expenditure; expenditure on major repairs; rental yields, capital gains, total returns and portfolio returns.

Charging rent

7.2 Some landlords were not charging rent for the most recent tenancy. One in eight lettings in the all lettings sample and one in 20 in the recent lettings sample were let rent free by the landlord (Table 7.1). While rent was being charged at the great majority of lettings, in some cases the amount involved was relatively nominal. In the all lettings sample, the lowest rent being charged was only £120 a year; in the recent lettings sample it was £12 a year. This reinforces the point that not all private landlords let accommodation in order to make a profit on the rent.

7.3 Not surprisingly, the average gross weekly rent for the most recent tenancy was higher in the recent lettings sample (£85) than in the all lettings sample (£68). However, there was a very considerable variation in rents within both samples. In these circumstances, the median is a better measure of the average rent than the mean because it is less affected by extreme values. The median weekly rent for the all lettings sample was £50, quite a bit lower than the mean rent, which was pushed upwards by a relatively small number of very large rents. The median rent for the recent lettings sample was £70 (Table 7.2).

Table 7.1 : Whether rent was charged for the most recent tenancy

	All lettings	Recent lettings
	%	%
Rent charged	84	93
Rent free	12	5
Don't know/refused	4	2
Total	**100**	**100**
(Base)	(301)	(512)

Base: all addresses

Table 7.2 : Gross weekly rents

	All lettings	Recent lettings
	£pw	£pw
Lower quartile	30	48
Median	50	70
Upper quartile	79	95
Mean	68	85
(Base)	(253)	(475)

Base: addresses where rent was being charged

7.4   As would be expected, in both samples, the mean rent varied considerably between the different letting types, being much higher for assured shorthold and, to a lesser extent, assured tenancies than for regulated tenancies. Rents also broadly increased in line with the respondent's estimate of the vacant possession values for the address (Table 7.3). Thus, there was a statistically significant and positive correlation between the rent for all lettings at the address and the estimated vacant possession value; this relationship was stronger in the all lettings sample than in the recent lettings sample (the correlation coefficients were +0.7 and +0.4 respectively).

7.5   Among addresses where the most recent tenancy had commenced before the implementation of rent deregulation in January 1989, 57% in the all lettings sample and 48% in the recent lettings sample, had a fair rent registered with the rent officer; 30% and 36% respectively had a rent that was privately agreed between the tenant and the landlord (or agent); while 13% and 17% respectively were rent free.

Table 7.3 : Average weekly rents by quintiles of estimated vacant possession value		
Estimated vacant possession value	All lettings	Recent lettings
	£pw	£pw
Less than £34K	42	57
£35K, less than £45K	54	64
£45K, less than £60K	61	69
£60K, less than £85K	69	84
£85K and above	138	140
All tenancies	68	85
(Base)	(232)	(407)
Base: addresses where rent was charged		

7.6   In 86% and 85% of cases respectively, it was the landlord or the agent, rather than the tenant or the local authority, that had applied for the *fair rent* to be registered on the last occasion. In the all lettings sample of addresses, 36% of fair rents had last been changed in 1993 or 1994, while 79% had last been changed in 1992 to 1994. In the recent lettings sample, 45% of fair rents had last been changed in 1993 or 1994 and 60% in 1992 to 1994. Thus there were very few fair rents that had remained the same for many years; most had been re-registered in the year or two prior to the survey or not long before then.

7.7   Among addresses where the rent on the most recent tenancy was *privately agreed* - including those that had commenced before January 1989 - 69% in the all lettings sample and 63% in the recent lettings sample, had adjusted the rent since the tenancy had commenced; 21% and 34% respectively had not adjusted the rent; and the remainder could not say if it had ever been adjusted on the most recent tenancy. Where rents had been adjusted, this had taken place in the relatively recent past. Thus 94% of privately agreed rents in the all lettings sample, and 98% in the recent lettings sample, had a rent that had last been adjusted in 1989 or later.

7.8   Where privately agreed rents had been adjusted, in 84% of cases in the all lettings sample and 85% of cases in the recent lettings sample, the adjustment had been upwards, while in 16% and 15% of cases respectively, the rent had been decreased. Thus whilst most rents had been increased, some had been decreased when the rent was last adjusted.

7.9   There was a considerable variation in the percentage by which rents had been increased but much less in the extent to which they had been decreased. A comparison of individual rent increases with the vacant possession values of the addresses suggested that the largest increases had occurred where the previous rent had been very low. While it was not possible from the survey to ascertain why these rents had been so low, it does suggest that the very large increases were cases where the rent had been adjusted up to the market level rather than reflecting a sharp increase in market rents.

7.10 In the all lettings sample the median *increase* in rent had been 12%, while in the recent lettings sample it had been 10%. The median *decreases* were six % and eight % respectively. In absolute terms, the median rent increase was £5 per week in the all lettings sample and £6 per week in the recent lettings sample. The mean increases were £10 and £16 respectively (Tables 7.4a and 7.4b).

Table 7.4a : Percentage increase or decrease when the rent was last adjusted

	All lettings		Recent lettings	
	Rent increased	Rent decreased	Rent increased	Rent decreased
	%	%	%	%
Lower quartile	+6.0	-4.2	+5.9	-4.3
Median	+11.6	-6.1	+10.0	-7.7
Upper quartile	+20.2	-12.5	+27.3	-13.2
Mean	+28.4	-12.2	+72.5	-12.3
(Base)	(78)	(15)	(197)	(33)

Base: all addresses where a privately arranged rent was being charged and where the rent had ever been changed

Table 7.4b : Monetary increase in weekly rent when the rent was last adjusted

	All lettings	Recent lettings
	£pw	£pw
Lower quartile	+£3	+£3
Median	+£5	+£6
Upper quartile	+£10	+£12
Mean	+£10	+£16
(Base)	(78)	(197)

Base: all addresses where a privately arranged rent was being charged and where the rent had been increased

7.11 Where the most recent tenancy had commenced on or after 15 January 1989, landlords and agents were asked whether, in deciding the rent for the accommodation, they set it at the maximum they thought they could get, at what they considered to be a reasonable amount, to cover their costs, or at some other level? Thirteen % of the all lettings sample and 19% of the recent lettings sample described their approach as being rent maximisation. The majority of both samples (53% and 64% respectively) said they set the rent at what they considered to be a 'reasonable' amount. Four % and six % respectively said they set the rent to cover their costs. Business and sideline landlords gave similar responses to this question, but institutional landlords were much more likely to say that the tenancy was rent free or cite some other criterion by which they set the rent.

What the rent was expected to cover

7.12 Landlords at addresses where rent was being charged were asked what they expected the rent to cover. The answers were broadly the same for both samples. The results confirm that the majority of private landlords were not primarily investment motivated, though they did want to cover their costs.

7.13 The great majority of landlords - 76% in the all lettings sample and 82% in the recent lettings sample - expected the rent to cover wear and tear and repairs. Most landlords also expected the rent to cover the insurance costs of the property (65% and 73% respectively). Four fifths of landlords in the all lettings sample and half in the recent lettings sample expected the rent to cover their management costs. However, a third or less of landlords expected the rent to cover any one of the other items. In both samples, roughly a fifth of landlords expected the rent to provide a return on the open market vacant possession value of the address and a similar proportion expected it to provide a return on the initial purchase price.

Table 7.5 : Items that the rent was expected to cover

Items	All lettings	Recent lettings
	%	%
Contribution to mortgage/loan	27	30
Repairs, wear and tear	76	82
Gas and electricity	11	10
Telephone bills	4	3
Council tax	8	15
Water rates/sewerage charges	26	33
Management costs	43	51
Insurance costs	65	73
Return on market value with vacant possession	20	21
Return on initial purchase price	22	23
Other	9	12
(Base)	(185)	(302)

Base: addresses where rent was being charged

7.14 Across both samples, there was a broadly similar pattern of responses between the three different landlord types about what the rent was expected to cover (Table 7.6). Sideline landlords were more likely than the others to expect the rent to cover the mortgage. Business and sideline investment landlords were much more likely than sideline noninvestment landlords and institutional landlords to expect the rent to provide either a return on the initial purchase price or the vacant possession value of the address. Institutional landlords were more likely than the others to expect the rent to cover costs such as gas and electricity, and water rates and sewage charges.

Table 7.6 : Items that the rent was expected to cover by type of landlord letting the address

Items	All lettings				Recent lettings		
	Business	Sideline		Instit-ution	Business	Sideline	Instit-ution
		Invest-ment	Non-invest-ment				
	%	%	%	%	%	%	%
Contribution to a mortgage/loan	13	29	36	7	12	36	26
Repairs, wear and tear	84	78	68	87	85	80	87
Gas and electricity	11	3	15	27	9	9	19
Telephone bills	3	3	6	7	2	3	3
Council tax	8	5	10	13	15	15	13
Water rates/sewerage charges	18	27	22	60	27	33	42
Management costs	58	41	33	60	58	43	90
Insurance costs	76	75	54	53	83	71	68
Return on market value with vacant possession	32	29	7	7	31	19	16
Return on initial purchase price	32	33	10	-	36	22	7
Other	3	3	12	33	6	12	19
(Base)	(38)	(63)	(69)	(15)	(59)	(211)	(31)

Base: addresses where rent was being charged

7.15 Having said what they expected the rent to cover, landlords were asked whether the rent from the most recent tenancy was sufficient to cover the items they had mentioned. Agents were also asked whether they thought the rent was sufficient. A much higher proportion of respondents in the recent lettings sample than in the all lettings sample thought that the rent was sufficient. In the all lettings sample, just under half thought the rent was sufficient, while a similar proportion thought it was insufficient. But in the recent lettings sample, seven out of 10 thought it was sufficient and only a quarter thought it insufficient (Table 7.7). In the all lettings sample, business landlords were no more likely than sideline landlords (49% and 51% respectively) to say the rent was sufficient, whereas in the recent lettings sample they were a little more likely to take that view (80% compared with 69%).

7.16 One reason why landlords and agents in the recent lettings sample were more likely to say that the rent was sufficient was the fact that, on average, they were taken out later than those in the all lettings sample. In the all lettings sample, if not in the recent lettings one, respondents where the most recent tenancy commenced after 14 January 1989 were much more likely than those where it commenced before 15 January 1989, to say that the rent was sufficient. Thus, in the all lettings sample, whereas respondents at three fifths of addresses where the tenancy commenced after 14 January 1989 thought the rent was sufficient, this was true of only a third of respondents where the tenancy was taken out before that date (Table 7.8).

Table 7.7 : Whether landlords and agents thought the rent from the most recent tenancy was sufficient

	All lettings	Recent lettings
	%	%
Sufficient	49	72
Not sufficient	47	24
Can't say	4	4
Total	**100**	**100**
(Base)	(241)	(401)

Base: addresses at which rent was being charged

Table 7.8 : Whether landlords and agents thought the rent from the most recent tenancy was sufficient, by date of tenancy

	All lettings		Recent lettings	
	Before 15 January 1989	After 14 January 1989	Before 15 January 1989	After 14 January 1989
	%	%	%	%
Sufficient	33	59	64	72
Not sufficient	66	35	36	23
Can't say	1	6	0	4
Total	**100**	**100**	**100**	**100**
(Base)	(97)	(143)	(33)	(368)

Base: addresses at which rent was being charged

7.17 In both samples, the rent being charged at addresses where it was considered to be sufficient was higher than where it was considered to be insufficient. Thus in the all lettings sample, the mean weekly rent where it was considered to be sufficient by the landlord or agent was £91, but only £50 were it was thought to be insufficient. Likewise, in the recent lettings sample, the mean rent where it was considered to be sufficient was £93, but only £72 where it was considered to be insufficient.

7.18 Landlords and agents who thought the rent was insufficient were asked what would be a sufficient rent for the tenancy. The average 'sufficient rent' was £78 per week in the all lettings sample and £112 a week in the recent lettings sample. Again, there was a considerable variation in sufficient rents. The median figures were £67 and £98 respectively.

7.19 Finally, the monthly rent of landlords who were buying the address with a mortgage were compared with the monthly repayments on the loan. As we saw in Chapter Three approximately a quarter of addresses in both samples were being purchased with a mortgage at the time of the survey. In the all lettings sample, the rent on about a third (32%) of addresses being bought with a mortgage was less than the mortgage repayments; in the recent lettings sample, this was true of about a quarter (24%) of addresses. A quarter of addresses with a mortgage (the lower quartile) had a deficit of rent after mortgage repayments of up to £48 per month in the all lettings sample and up to £10 per month in the recent lettings sample. On average, however, the rent was in excess of the monthly mortgage repayments: the median was a 'surplus' of £78 per month in the all lettings sample and £115 per month in the recent lettings sample. The upper quartile figures were a surplus of £224 and £315 respectively.

Rent arrears and voids

7.20 Including in the total addresses that were rent free, 11% of privately rented addresses had rent that was uncollected in the all lettings sample, as did 14% in the recent lettings sample. At 78% and 79% of addresses respectively, the landlord or agent was able to collect all of the rent (Table 7.9).

Table 7.9 : Whether the landlord/agent was able to collect all of the rent due over the past 12 months on the letting		
	All lettings	Recent lettings
	%	%
Collected all of rent	78	79
Did not collect all of the rent	11	14
Rent free/not applicable	10	5
Don't know	*	2
Total	**100**	**100**
(Base)	(301)	(507)
Base: all addresses including rent-free		

7.21 Not surprisingly, the percentage of addresses where all of the rent was collected was higher when rent free addresses are excluded from the figures. Thus landlords or their agents were able to collect all of the rent due on the letting over the past twelve months on 87% of *addresses where rent was being charged* in the all lettings sample and 85% of such addresses in the recent lettings sample. In other words, some rent was uncollected at 13% and 15% of addresses respectively in the two samples. A higher proportion of furnished than unfurnished addresses had rent that was uncollected. Thus in the all lettings sample, some rent was uncollected at 21% of addresses let furnished compared with seven % let unfurnished. In the recent lettings sample the difference was less great: there was uncollected rent at 19% of furnished and 12% of unfurnished addresses (Table 7.10).

Table 7.10 : Rent uncollected in the past 12 months	All lettings	Recent lettings
	%	%
% of lettings in arrears:		
-furnished	21	19
-unfurnished	7	15
-all	13	15
(Base)	(253)	(460)
Base: addresses where rent was charged		
Arrears as % of rent due on lettings in arrears:		
-furnished	15.1	14.6
-unfurnished	26.1	14.0
-all	18.9	14.4
(Base)	(29)	(67)
Base: lettings where rent was uncollected		
Arrears as % of rent due averaged across all lettings		
-furnished	3.2	2.7
-unfurnished	1.9	1.7
-all	2.4	2.2
(Base)	(253)	(460)
Base: addresses where rent was charged		

7.22 The mean amount of uncollected rent was £989 in the all lettings sample and £825 in the recent lettings sample. The medians were lower than the mean in both samples, at £450 and £567 respectively.

7.23 On average, the amount of rent uncollected in the previous 12 months was equivalent to 18.9% of the rent currently due at those addresses in the all lettings sample and 14.4% of those addresses in the recent lettings sample. In the all lettings sample, at a quarter of all lettings the landlord or agent failed to collect 4.6% or less of the rent, while at the other extreme, a quarter did not collect 25% or more; the median percentage was 10.9%. In the recent lettings sample, a quarter of all lettings had landlords or agents that did not collect 3.5% or less of the rent; while at the other extreme, a quarter of addresses had landlords or agents that were unable to collect 20% or more of the rent; the median was 8.3%.

7.24 In the all lettings sample the amount of rent uncollected as a percentage of the current rent was higher among unfurnished than among furnished tenancies, whereas in the recent lettings sample it was the other way around. If these rent arrears percentages are averaged across all of the addresses in each sample, they account for 2.4% in the all lettings sample and 2.2% in the recent lettings sample (Table 7.10).

7.25 Including in the total rent free dwellings, *rent was lost due to vacancies* on 15% of addresses in the all lettings sample and as many as 42% of addresses in the recent lettings sample (Table 7.11). Again, these figures are a little higher when rent free addresses are excluded from the figures. Thus, in the all lettings sample, 17% of addresses at which rent was charged lost some rent due to vacancies, compared with 45% in the recent lettings sample (Table 7.12).

Table 7.11 : Whether there was any loss of rent on the letting over the past 12 months due to vacancies

	All lettings	Recent lettings
	%	%
Rent not lost	78	52
Rent lost	15	42
Rent free/not applicable	7	4
Don't know	-	2
Total	**100**	**100**
(Base)	(300)	(510)

Base: all addresses including rent-free

Table 7.12 : Rent lost due to vacancies in the past 12 months		All lettings	Recent lettings
		%	%
% of lettings with rent lost due to vacancies			
-furnished		32	45
-unfurnished		7	45
-all		17	45
(Base)		(252)	(463)
Base: addresses where rent was charged			
Rent lost as % of rent due on lettings with vacancies:			
-furnished		13.7	10.7
-unfurnished		10.8	17.4
-all		12.9	13.9
(Base)		(3)	(193)
Base: addresses where rent was lost due to vacancies			
Rent lost as % of rent due averaged across all lettings			
-furnished		4.4	5.1
-unfurnished		0.8	7.8
-all		2.3	6.4
(Base)		(252)	(463)
Base: addresses where rent was charged			

7.26 In the all lettings sample, the percentage of lettings which lost rent due to vacancies was nearly four times as high among furnished lettings as among unfurnished ones. This is hardly surprising since tenant turnover in the furnished sub-sector is much higher than in the unfurnished sub-sector and, hence, there are more likely to be periods when the property is in empty in between lettings. Yet in the recent lettings sample, the percentage of lettings with rent lost because of vacancies was the same for furnished and unfurnished tenancies.

7.27 Thus not only was the level of vacancies much higher in the recent lettings sample than in the all lettings sample, but the difference was especially great among unfurnished tenancies. This suggests there may be some over supply of unfurnished lettings coming onto the market, perhaps because of the emergence of property slump lettings. As we shall see in chapter nine, this is to some extent borne out by comments among a minority of respondents about the increased competition for tenants since 1988.

7.28 The mean amount of rent lost as a result of vacancies in the previous 12 months was £793 in the all lettings sample and £765 in the recent lettings sample. The median rent loss was £375 in the all lettings sample and £533 in the recent lettings sample.

7.29 Expressed in percentage terms, rent lost due to voids was equivalent to 12.9% of the current annual rent in the all lettings sample and 13.9% in the recent lettings sample. The distribution of losses was similar across the two samples. The median amount of rent lost was 8.3% in both samples. A quarter of addresses in the all lettings sample lost 4.4% or less of the rent, while a similar proportion lost 4.8% or less in the recent lettings sample. A quarter of addresses lost 16.7% or more of the rent in the all lettings sample and 16.8% or more in the recent lettings sample. If these figures are averaged across all addresses at which rent was charged in each of the samples, they accounted for 2.2% and 6.4% respectively (Table 6.12).

Management and maintenance

7.30 Landlords and agents were asked to give details of the management and maintenance running costs over the past 12 months: 62% in the all lettings sample and 57% in the recent lettings sample were able and willing to do so. These costs have to be treated with some care: in 75% and 76% of cases respectively, the figure were estimates rather than exact figures. Moreover, some landlords are better at accounting for their expenditure than others. In addition, previous research (Crook and Martin, 1988) has suggested that private individual landlords do not always cost - or recognise as a cost - the time which they spend undertaking management and maintenance activities on their lettings.

7.31 The mean management and maintenance expenditure over the previous twelve months was £1,019 (£20 pw) in the all lettings sample and £1,758 (£34 pw) in the recent lettings sample. The median figures were much lower at £520 and £800 respectively. In the all lettings sample, 25% of landlords and agents had spent up to £300, while at the other extreme 25% of them had spent at least £1,000 on management and maintenance in the previous twelve months. In the recent lettings sample, at 25% of addresses, up to £300 had been spent, while at the other extreme £1,500 or more had been spent by the 25% of addresses in the upper quartile (Table 7.13).

Table 7.13 : Management and maintenance costs over the past 12 months	All lettings	Recent lettings
	£	£
Lower quartile	300	500
Median	520	800
Upper quartile	1,000	1,500
Mean	1,019	1,758
(Base)	(178)	(275)
Base: all addresses		

7.32 There was a statistically significant, positive relationship between the *absolute amount* of money spent on management and maintenance and the annual rent for all lettings at the sampled address; this relationship was less strong in the all lettings sample than in the recent lettings sample (the correlation coefficients were +0.5 and +0.9 respectively). That is to say, the larger the rent, the larger the amount of money spent on management and maintenance at the address (Table 6.14). However, there was no correlation between the annual rent for all lettings at the sampled address and the *percentage* of the rent which was devoted to management and maintenance.

7.33 Management and maintenance costs on average accounted for 30% of the rent in the all lettings sample and 26% in the rent lettings sample. The median figures were lower at 19% and 20% respectively (Table 7.15). In the all lettings sample, the percentage of rent accounted for by management and maintenance was higher in the furnished sub-sector (36%) than in the unfurnished sub-sector (27%); whereas, in the recent letting sample, they were the same (26%) for both sub-sectors.

Table 7.14 : Annual management and maintenance costs by quintiles of gross annual rent for all tenancies at the address

Gross annual rent	All lettings	Most recent lettings
	£pw	£pw
Less than £2,080	568	412
£2,080 to £3,483	569	717
£3,432 to £4,199	620	1,113
£4,200 to £6,503	1,074	1,136
£6,504 and above	3,279	4,377
All tenancies	1,019	1,758
(Base)	(178)	(275)

Base: addresses where rent was charged

Table 7.15 : Management and maintenance costs over the past 12 months as a percentage of the annual rent

	All lettings	Recent lettings
	%	%
Lower quartile	10	12
Median	19	20
Upper quartile	32	32
Mean	30	26
(Base)	(155)	(225)

Base: addresses where rent was changed

Major repairs and improvements

7.34 This section looks at the extent to which landlords carried out major building work on sample dwellings. The survey did not cover the type of work done in great detail, because repair and maintenance by private landlords was the subject of a separate research project commissioned by the Building Research Division of the Department of the Environment (Crook, Henneberry & Hughes, 1995). Because the current survey did not collect information about the physical condition of the sampled dwellings, it is not possible to show how far landlords' spending on major works was directed at the addressees in the worst condition and how far spending remedied the disrepair at other addresses. Nevertheless, the current survey was used to establish what proportion of the two samples had been the subject of major works, how much had been spent, how it was financed and the extent to which, in the landlords' and agents' opinions, work was currently required at them.

7.35 Landlords and agents were asked if any major repairs, improvements or conversion work had been done by the landlord at the address since 1980 (or later in the case of those acquired, or coming into the landlords' possession, after 1980). For these purposes major works were defined as either structural repair work (like roof replacement) or improvement (like putting in central heating or a new bathroom) or conversion (such as adding on a new extension or turning a house into flats).

Table 7.16 : Major works done to sample addresses since 1980

Work done	All lettings managed by:			Recent lettings managed by:		
	Landlord	Agent	All	Landlord	Agent	All
	%	%	%	%	%	%
Yes	64	34	55	67	44	59
No	35	58	42	31	43	35
Don't know	1	8	3	1	13	5
Total	**100**	**100**	**100**	**100**	**100**	**100**
(Base)	(212)	(89)	(301)	(331)	(181)	(512)

Base: all addresses

Table 7.17 : Major work done to sample addresses since 1980 by number of lettings at address

Work done	All lettings		Recent lettings	
	1 only	1 +	1 only	1 +
	%	%	%	%
Yes	52	75	54	82
No	44	25	46	18
Don't know	4	-	-	-
Total	**100**	**100**	**100**	**100**
(Base)	(269)	(32)	(425)	(87)

Base: all addresses

7.36 As Table 7.16 shows, landlords had done work to 55% of the addresses in the sample of all lettings and to 59% of the recent lettings. It should be noted that a greater proportion had work done where they were managed by the landlords themselves, and not by the agents (partly because agents did not know whether such work had been done to the recent lettings). Not unexpectedly, where the addresses had more than one letting, a greater proportion of addresses had works done (Table 7.17).

7.37 There were some variations in the extent to which work had been done by different types of landlords. For example, work had been done to a greater proportion of addresses belonging to sideline landlords who regarded the addresses as investments and to those belonging to business landlords than to those belonging to other landlords (Table 7.18). Moreover, work had been done to a greater proportion of addresses belonging to medium sized landlords (owning between two and 40 lettings throughout England) than to those owned by others (Table 7.19). There were no statistically significant differences in the incidence of major improvement work between addresses where the landlord was or had been resident and those where they had never been resident there.

Table 7.18 : Major work done to sample addresses by landlord type

Work done	All lettings				Recent lettings			
	Sideline landlords		Business	Institution	Sideline landlords		Business	Institution
	Non-investment	Investment			Non-investment	Investment		
	%	%	%	%	%	%	%	%
Yes	61	70	65	54	67	72	78	35
No	36	30	35	45	32	28	22	57
Don't know	4	-	-	1	1	-	-	8
Total	**100**	**100**	**100**	**100**	**100**	**100**	**100**	**100**
(Base)	(84)	(66)	(40)	(22)	(113)	(118)	(63)	(37)

Base: all addresses where landlord interviewed

Table 7.19 : Major work done to sample addresses by size of landlord (total lettings in England)

Work done	All lettings				Recent lettings			
	Size of landlord:				Size of landlord:			
	1	2-7	8-40	41+	1	2-7	8-40	41+
	%	%	%	%	%	%	%	%
Yes	53	78	67	58	61	81	69	58
No/Don't know	47	22	33	42	39	19	31	42
Total	**100**	**100**	**100**	**100**	**100**	**100**	**100**	**100**
(Base)	(47)	(51)	(45)	(69)	(91)	(81)	(78)	(81)

Base: all addresses where landlord interviewed

7.38 By excluding addresses acquired after 1980, those which were currently their landlords' homes, and those which had once been their landlords' home (unless letting started after 1980), it is possible to get a more accurate estimate of the scale of major work that had taken place since 1980. Table 7.20 shows that two thirds of all lettings and two thirds of recent lettings which were in their landlords' ownership in 1980 had major work done to them at some time since then. Thus there is evidence of major works having been done at a large proportion of the addresses over the last 15 years.

7.39 Approximately half the work that had been done at all addresses at some time since 1980 had all been carried out in the same year, with the rest spread over several years. This complicates the estimate of how much landlords had spent because, without knowing how much was spent in each year, it is impossible to make an accurate estimate of the cost of work in real prices. Table 7.21 is based therefore on expenditure in 1994 prices for that part of the sample where the major work was all done in one year. In these cases it was possible to apply a building cost deflator to enable the 1994 price of the work to be estimated.

Table 7.20 : Major work done to addresses acquired by landlords before 1980 and who have not lived at the address since 1980		
Work done	All lettings	Recent lettings
	%	%
Yes	66	67
No	32	30
Don't know	2	4
Total	**100**	**100**
(Base)	(102)	(159)

Base: all addresses acquired by landlords before 1980

7.40 Table 7.21 shows that, where the major work had been carried out within one year, landlords had spent very nearly £7,000 in 1994 prices. The median costs in 1994 prices suggest that there was a substantial variation in the spending on those addresses where major work had been done since 1980. For example, in 1994 prices, over £9,937 had been spent at a quarter of the addresses with the sample of all lettings, but £1,770 or less at another quarter.

Table 7.21 : Average expenditure on major works (1994 prices)

	All lettings		Recent lettings	
	Per address	Per letting	Per address	Per letting
	£	£	£	£
Mean	6,999	5,926	11,053	7899
Lower quartile	1,770	1,295	2,056	1,625
Median	4,228	4,125	5,000	3,500
Upper quartile	9,937	8,115	14,720	10,875
(Base)	(60)	(60)	(99)	(99)

Base: addresses where work done and landlord interviewed and where work done within same year

Table 7.22 : Grants received for major work

(a) Whether grant received			All lettings		Recent lettings	
			%		%	
Grant received			17		14	
No grant received			80		81	
Don't know			3		5	
Total			**100**		**100**	
(Base)			(165)		(303)	
(b) Amount of grant received			£	(Base)	£	(Base)
Addresses where work was done within same year						
Average 94 price			5,077	(14)	9,721	(26)
Median 94 price			4,524	(14)	6,729	(26)

Base: addresses where major work done and where landlord interviewed

7.41 Quite high proportions of this expenditure were financed with the help of a grant. Seventeen percent of the work done to all lettings had received grant aid, as had 14% of the work done to recent lettings (Table 7.22). Looking just at addresses where major work had been done since 1989 (in those cases where the work was all done within the same year), when the grant regime last changed, four % of all lettings (and nine % of recent lettings) had received a grant. As Table 7.21 also shows, the average grant paid to all lettings where the work had been done within a year was just over £5,000 in 1994 prices. Whilst grants were received for only a minority of addresses where major work had been done, it accounted for an average of 57% of the total expenditure at those addresses.

Table 7.23 : Sources of finance for major work by type of landlords						
	All lettings			Recent lettings		
	Individual	Co/other	All	Individual	Co/other	All
	%	%	%	%	%	%
Borrowing	16	10	13	21	8	16
Personal savings	81	5	46	81	9	56
Company Capital	4	63	31	4	73	28
Other	5	27	15	2	13	6
Don't know	1	-	<1	-	1	<1
Total	**100**	**100**	**100**	**100**	**100**	**100**
(Base)	(73)	(62)	(135)	(145)	(78)	(223)

Base: addresses where major work done and landlord interviewed

Table 7.24 : Average borrowing for major work		
In 1994 prices	All lettings	Recent lettings
	£	£
Mean	8,287	12,836
Median	2,750	6,250

Base: addresses where money borrowed for major work and landlords interviewed

7.42 Landlords borrowed very little to finance major work. Only 13% of the work done to all lettings and 16% of the work done to recent lettings involved borrowing (Table 7.23). The pattern is very similar, whether addresses were owned by individual landlords or by companies and other organisations. Very little of the major work was financed by borrowing, most coming from landlords' personal savings (in the case of individual landlords) or from company capital (in the case of other landlords). As Table 7.24 shows, in 1994 prices landlords borrowed an average of £8,287 for works done to all lettings and £12,836 for work done at addresses with recent lettings. Although borrowing was incurred at very few addresses, it constituted 67% of expenditure on major work, when incurred.

7.43 The landlords and agents said that major work was needed at nearly one in five of all addresses. Where there was more than one letting, nearly three in 10 addresses needed major repairs, improvement or conversion work doing to it. The same proportion of addresses where there had been major work at some time since 1980 needed major work in 1994 as those where there had not been any major work (Table 7.25).

Table 7.25 : Whether major work done to address since 1980 by whether landlord or agent thought work needed in 1994

	All lettings				Recent lettings			
	Work done since 1980:				Work done since 1980:			
	Yes	No	DK	All	Yes	No	DK	All
	%	%	%	%	%	%	%	%
Yes	19	19	20	19	22	10	11	17
No	78	79	40	77	77	88	78	81
Don't know	3	2	40	4	1	2	11	1
Total	**100**	**100**	**100**	**100**	**100**	**100**	**100**	**100**
(Base)	(165)	(126)	(10)	(301)	(303)	(182)	(27)	(512)

Base: all addresses

Rental yields

7.44 Landlords and agents were asked to estimate the vacant possession market value of the addresses. Using these estimates it was possible to estimate rental yields on lettings for which a rent was being charged. The gross rental yield is defined here to mean the annual rent as a percentage of the estimated vacant possession value. Since the latter data were necessarily estimates, the resultant figures are referred to here as estimated rental yields.

7.45 The mean rental yields were 6.3% in the all lettings sample and 8.4% in the recent lettings sample. There was considerable variation in yields around this average, though the median yields (5.7% and 8.3% respectively) in both samples were not very different from the mean. In the all lettings sample, a quarter of addresses (the lower quartile) had yields of 2.6% or less, while at the other extreme, another quarter (the upper quartile) had yields of 9.2% or more. In the recent lettings sample, the lower quartile yield was 4.8%, while the upper quartile yield was 10.8% (Table 7.26).

Table 7.26 : Estimated gross rental yields	All lettings	Recent lettings
	%	%
Lower quartile	2.6	4.8
Median	5.7	8.3
Upper quartile	9.2	10.8
Mean	6.3	8.4
(Base)	(267)	(431)
Base: addresses where rent was charged		

7.46 Moreover, as is clear from Table 7.27, there was considerable variation around the average between different tenancy and landlord types. The average yield was about twice as high on tenancies taken out since January 1989 than on those taken out before then. This difference is mainly due to assured shortholds in the all lettings sample but to both assured and assured shortholds in the recent letting sample. As other surveys have found (Crook and Martin 1988; Kemp and Rhodes, 1994) the average gross yield on furnished lettings was higher than on unfurnished lettings.

Table 7.27 : Average estimated gross rental yields	All lettings	Recent lettings
	%	%
Before 15 January 1989	3.6	3.0
After 14 January 1989	8.0	8.9
Furnished	8.9	9.6
Unfurnished	4.8	7.0
Assured	5.2	8.6
Assured shorthold	9.0	9.2
Regulated	4.9	5.5
Other	4.7	6.3
Business	7.2	9.9
Sideline investment	7.3	9.6
Sideline noninvestment	5.2	6.0
Institution	2.1	5.5
Growth seeker	5.8	8.0
Income seeker	8.8	10.0

Slump victim	..	8.7
Employer	1.1	3.0
Other landlord	5.7	7.1
Agent respondent	6.9	8.7
All addresses	6.3	8.4

Base: addresses where rent was charged

7.47 In both samples, the average estimated yield being obtained by business and sideline investor landlords was higher than that being obtained by sideline noninvestor landlords. Especially in the all lettings sample, institutional landlords were obtaining lower yields on average than other types of landlord; this mainly reflected the preponderance of employers among institutional landlords. Income seeker landlords (that is, those who mainly viewed the letting as a source of rental income) were on average obtaining a gross rental yield that was two percentage points higher than growth seekers (those who mainly regarded the letting for its capital growth potential). In both samples, lettings managed by agents had a gross rental yield that was similar to the average.

7.48 There was a statistically significant but weak relationship between the annual rent and rental yields. In both samples, an analysis of gross yields by quintile of the annual rent for all lettings at the address suggested that the relationship between the two was nonlinear. The lowest yields were on addresses in the bottom (first) rent quintile, while the highest yields were in the upper (fifth) rent quintiles. But while yields in the third quintile were higher than in the second, they were lower than in the fourth quintile (Table 7.28).

Table 7.28 : Gross rental yields by quintiles of gross annual rent for all tenancies at the address		
Rent quintile	All lettings	Recent lettings
	%	%
Less than £2,080	3.9	3.2
£2,080 to £3,431	7.4	8.0
£3,432 to £4,199	9.8	9.7
£4,200 to £6,503	9.0	9.2
£6,504 and above	11.4	11.4

Base: addresses where rent was charged

7.49 A more linear relationship was found between gross yields and quintiles of vacant possession values. The highest yields were among the lowest value properties, while the lowest yields were found among the highest value properties (Table 6.29). However, while there was a statistically significant, inverse relationship (at the 95% confidence level) between gross rental yields and estimated vacant possession values, the strength of this relationship was fairly weak.

Table 7.29 : Gross rental yields by quintiles for estimated vacant possession values		
Estimated vacant possession value quintile	All lettings	Recent lettings
	% pa	% pa
Less than £35K	8.6	12.7
£35k less than £45k	7.0	8.9
£45k less than £60k	6.4	7.6
£60k less than £85k	5.1	7.7
£85k and above	4.2	6.3
Base: addresses where rent was charged		

7.50 Net rental yields were calculated by deducting management and maintenance costs in the previous 12 months from the annual rent for all lettings at the address and then computing this net rent as a percentage of estimated vacant possession values. The average estimated net yield was 5.5% in the all lettings sample and 6.8% in the recent lettings sample. Once again, however, there was considerable variation around these two averages. The median net yield was 4.8% in the all lettings sample and 6.4% in the recent lettings sample. The lower quartile net yields were 2.6 % and 4.1%; the upper quartile net yields were 7.9% and 8.8% respectively (Table 7.30).

Table 7.30 : Estimated net yield		
	All lettings	Recent lettings
	%	%
Lower quartile	2.6	4.1
Median	4.8	6.4
Upper quartile	7.9	8.8
Mean	5.5	6.8
(Base)	(146)	(228)
Base: addresses where rent was charged		

Table 7.31 : Estimated net rental yields		
Type of tenancy/landlord	All lettings	Recent lettings
	% pa	% pa
Before 15 January 1989	3.4	3.7
After 14 January 1989	6.5	7.1
Furnished	6.8	8.0
Unfurnished	4.6	5.4
Business	5.2	7.9
Sideline investment	6.0	7.7
Sideline noninvestment	5.3	5.3
Institution	..	..
Growth seeker	4.5	7.0
Income seeker	7.1	8.0
Slump victim	..	7.0
Employer	..	..
Other landlord	5.0	5.7
Agent respondent	5.6	6.5
All addresses	5.5	6.8

Base: addresses where rent was charged

7.51 As with gross yields, net yields were about twice as high on tenancies taken out on or later than 15 January 1989 than on those taken out before that date. Despite higher management and maintenance costs, furnished tenancies had a higher net yield than unfurnished tenancies (Table 7.31).

7.52 Since not all landlords or their agents regarded the rent from the address as sufficient, the amount of rent which they said would be sufficient was used to calculate a gross 'sufficient yield'. In the all lettings sample, the average sufficient yield was 8.8%; in the recent lettings sample it was 12.5%. The median sufficient yields were 7.7% and 11.3% respectively. The lower quartile sufficient yield was 5.2% in the all lettings sample and 8.0% in the recent lettings sample; the upper quartile net yields were 11.5% and 13.4% (Table 7.32).

Table 7.32 : Estimated 'sufficient' yield	All lettings	Recent lettings
	%	%
Lower quartile	5.2	8.0
Median	7.7	11.2
Upper quartile	11.5	13.4
Mean	8.8	12.5
(Base)	(104)	(83)
Base: addresses where rent was regarded as insufficient		

7.53 Not only were gross yields higher on tenancies taken out on or after 15 January 1989 than those taken out before that date, but so too were gross sufficient yields. In the all lettings sample, the sufficient yield was 10.2% on post 14 January 1989 tenancies and 7.5% on pre 15 January 1989 tenancies. In the recent lettings sample, the difference was even greater: 13.2% compared with 4.2% respectively. The sufficient yield on furnished tenancies was higher than that on unfurnished tenancies in the all lettings sample, but in the recent lettings sample it was the other way around (Table 7.33).

Table 7.33 : Estimated 'sufficient' gross yields		
Type of tenancy/landlord	All lettings	Recent lettings
	% pa	% pa
Before 15 January 1989	7.5	4.2
After 14 January 1989	10.2	13.2
Furnished	11.9	14.1
Unfurnished	7.7	10.6
All tenancies	8.8	12.5
(Base)	(104)	(83)
Base: addresses where the rent was regarded as insufficient		

Table 7.34 : Estimated 'yield gap'	All lettings	Recent lettings
	%	%
Lower quartile	1.4	1.5
Median	2.9	2.7
Upper quartile	4.8	4.6
Mean	3.6	4.1
(Base)	(104)	(83)

Base: addresses where the rent was regarded as insufficient

7.54 The sufficient yields were compared with the actual yields that were being achieved to compute a 'yield gap' for addresses where the landlord or the agent regarded the rent as being insufficient. It should be stressed that this 'yield gap' is not necessarily the amount which these landlords regarded as sufficient to persuade them to keep letting the address nor to induce them to invest in additional properties. It is simply the difference between the yield which these landlords were obtaining and the yield which is implied by the rent which they said would meet their expectations regarding the items which they felt the rent should cover.

7.55 The average yield gap was 3.6% in the all lettings sample and 4.1% in the recent lettings sample. The medians were 2.9% and 2.7% respectively. The lower quartile yield gaps were 1.4% and 1.5%, while the upper quartiles were 4.8% and 4.6% respectively (Table 7.34). However, the average yield gap varied relatively little between different categories of letting and landlord in each sample (Table 7.35).

Table 7.35 : Estimated 'yield gap' where the current yield was regarded as insufficient		
Type of tenancy/motive	All lettings	Recent lettings
	% pa	% pa
Before 15 January 1989	3.6	..
After 14 January 1989	3.6	4.3
Furnished	3.8	4.2
Unfurnished	3.6	4.0
Investment motive	3.5	5.0
Other motive	3.9	4.6
All addresses	3.6	4.1

Base: addresses where the rent was insufficient

Capital gains 7.56 As well as rental income, residential housing to let has the potential to achieve capital gains, though as the experience since 1988 has shown it can also lead to capital losses. In fact, in the all lettings sample 19% of addresses and in the recent lettings sample 13% of addresses, had experienced a *nominal* fall in value when purchase prices are compared with estimated vacant possession values.

7.57 Among addresses which had experienced a capital loss in *real terms* (that is, adjusted by the retail price index) the average fall was 5.3% per annum in the all lettings sample and 5.4% per annum in the recent lettings sample. Among addresses that had experienced a capital gain in real terms, the average increase was 13.3% per annum in the all lettings sample and 12.7% per annum in the recent lettings sample.

7.58 There was very considerable variation in real capital gains and losses. Including addresses where there had been a real loss, the average capital gain was 5.4% in the all lettings sample and 7.1% in the recent lettings sample. Because of the presence of some very extreme capital gains, the median is probably the better guide to the average capital gain. The median for the all lettings sample was 1.8% while the median for the recent lettings sample was 3.4% per annum (Table 7.36). Investment motivated landlords in both samples had experienced a mean capital gain that was approximately three times that of landlords who mainly had other motives for letting the address.

Table 7.36 : Real capital gains per annum		
	All lettings	Recent lettings
	%	%
Lower quartile	-3.5	-2.3
Median	1.8	3.4
Upper quartile	10.0	7.4
Mean	5.4	7.1
(Base)	(90)	(156)

Base: addresses which had been purchased

7.59 As Table 7.37 shows, addresses which had been acquired in the period from 1980 to 1988 had the highest median capital gain, while those acquired in the period from 1989 to 1994 had the lowest rates of capital gain. Indeed, in the all lettings sample, the median annual capital gain was negative at -2.4%; in other words, on average owners had made a capital loss in real terms. There was a small number of cases among the addresses acquired since 1988 where the owner had made a very high rate of annual capital gain. Inspection of the purchase price, estimated vacant possession value, rents and yield data suggests that these very high figures were due to landlords purchasing the property

(often, but not in all cases, tenanted) at well below its vacant possession market value.

7.60 Particularly in the all lettings sample, landlords who had acquired the property vacant had experienced a lower rate of capital growth than those who had acquired the address with sitting tenants. This is not surprising because, in general, since the first world war residential property with sitting tenants has traded at a discount from vacant possession values. Hence landlords who purchase tenanted property can make a capital gain if they can sell it with vacant possession even if property values have not changed since it was acquired.

Table 7.37 : Median real capital gain per annum by date at which the address was acquired		
Date acquired	All lettings	Recent lettings
	%	%
Before 1980	1.2	3.4
1980 to 1988	2.8	5.2
1989 to 1990	-2.4	2.0
All addresses	1.8	3.4
(Base)	(90)	(156)
Base: addresses which had been purchased		

7.61 When the respondents' estimate of the sitting tenant value for the address was computed as a percentage of the mean vacant possession value, the mean was 66% in the all lettings sample and 73% in the recent lettings sample. The median figures were only a little lower at 64% and 69% respectively (Table 7.38). In both samples the estimated mean sitting tenant value was substantially higher as a percentage of the vacant possession value on properties where the most recent tenancy commenced after the Housing Act came into force in January 1989 than on lettings taken out before that date. The mean percentage for deregulated tenancies was 74% in both samples, while for pre-January 1989 tenancies the mean was 57% in the all lettings sample and 55% in the recent lettings sample. This suggests that deregulation has helped to reduce the sitting tenant discount on residential tenancies to about a quarter of the dwelling value.

7.62 In monetary terms, the mean difference between vacant possession and sitting tenant values was £21,000 in both samples, while the median difference was £15,000 in both samples. This suggests that the property dealing strategy of buying tenanted properties and selling them once they become vacant - which has been an important component of the decline of private renting - remains a potentially profitable one, though less so than before deregulation.

Table 7.38 : Estimated sitting tenant value as a percentage of estimated vacant possession value

	All lettings	Recent lettings
	%	%
Lower quartile	50	50
Median	64	69
Upper quartile	82	90
Mean	66	73
(Base)	(153)	(262)

Base: addresses which had been purchased

Total returns

7.63 Total returns were calculated as the sum of the rental yield and the annualized capital gain. This definition is thus based on the *current* rental yield and the annual rate of capital gain *since the address was acquired*; if the capital gain or loss over the *previous year* had been used instead of the rate since the address was acquired, the total return figures would have come out rather differently and, in fact, much lower, since house prices in England fell in real terms during the year prior to the survey.

7.64 Two rates of total return were calculated: a *gross* total return based on the gross rental yield and the annualised, real capital gain; and the *net* total return based on the net rental yield and the annualised, real capital gain. As Table 7.39 shows, within both samples there was very considerable variation gross and net total returns. The median gross total return was 9.7% in the all lettings sample and 11.7% in the recent lettings sample. The median net total returns were 6.3% and 9.8% respectively.

Table 7.39 : Gross and net total rate of return

	All lettings		Recent lettings	
	Gross	Net	Gross	Net
	%	%	%	%
Lower quartile	3.2	1.7	6.3	4.3
Median	9.7	6.3	11.7	9.8
Upper quartile	18.4	17.8	19.7	16.3
Mean	13.1	11.2	16.7	12.3
(Base)	(90)	(51)	(156)	(98)

Base: addresses which had been purchased and at which rent was charged

Portfolio returns

7.65 Landlords were asked whether they thought the rental income from all of their lettings was sufficient to cover all necessary repairs and give a reasonable return. Although a higher proportion of landlords in the recent lettings sample than in the all lettings sample considered the rental income from their lettings portfolio to be sufficient (47% compared with 39%) the differences between the two samples were not statistically significant. Combining the two samples, the proportion of landlords who thought their rental income was sufficient was about the same as the proportion who thought it was not sufficient (44% and 43%), while one in eight (13%) said they did not want a return or gave some other response along those lines (Table 7.40).

Table 7.40 : Whether landlords regarded the rent from all of their lettings as sufficient to cover all necessary repairs and give a reasonable return, by type of landlord

| | Business | Sideline | | Institution | All landlords |
		Invest-ment	Non-investment		
	%	%		%	%
Sufficient	60	62	24	26	44
Not sufficient	35	37	58	28	43
Don't want a return	3	2	13	42	10
Other	2	-	6	4	3
Total	**100**	**100**	**100**	**100**	**100**
(Base)	(102)	(182)	(191)	(57)	(553)

Base: addresses which had been purchased and where rent was charged

7.66 As in many other areas, the views of business and sideline investor landlords were similar to each other but different from the other two categories of landlord. Where the letting was owned by a business or sideline investor landlord, a far higher proportion than of other landlords expressed the view that their rental income was sufficient. Among lettings owned by institutional landlords a far higher proportion than of others said they did not want a return. Thus among lettings owned by business landlords and sideline investor landlords, three out of five said their rental income was sufficient, compared with about a quarter of those owned by sideline non investor and institutional landlords. Relatively few lettings were owned by either business or sideline investor landlords who did not want a return (three % and two % respectively) but one in eight (13%) sideline investor landlords and two fifths (42%) of institutional landlords gave this response (Table 7.40).

7.67 Lettings where the landlord was an income seeker, and to a lesser extent those where the landlord was a growth seeker, were more likely than other landlords to say their rental income was sufficient to cover repairs and give a reasonable return. Thus investment motivated landlords were more likely than others to think their rental income was sufficient. Lettings owned by slump landlords were more likely than others to regard their rental income as insufficient (moreover, their portfolio was often only one letting), while those owned by employer landlords were the most likely to say that they were not seeking a return on their portfolio (Table 7.41).

	Growth seeker	Income seeker	Slump landlord	Employer	Other	All landlords
	%	%	%	%	%	%
Sufficient	49	68	33	16	26	44
Not sufficient	45	32	58	39	54	43
Don't want a return	3	1	8	36	16	10
Other	3	-	-	10	4	3
Total	**100**	**100**	**100**	**100**	**100**	**100**
(Base)	(97)	(183)	(24)	(62)	(166)	(532)

Table 7.41 : Whether landlords regarded the rent from all of their lettings as sufficient to cover all necessary repairs and give a reasonable return, by letting motive

Base: all addresses

8 Housing Benefit

Summary

- almost all landlords and agents had heard of Housing Benefit;

- landlords and agents at seven out of 10 addresses said that at least one of their current tenants was receiving Housing Benefit;

- the majority of landlords who were not currently letting to Housing Benefit recipients had done so in the past;

- only about one in 20 addresses had a landlord or agent who said they preferred to let their accommodation to tenants on Housing Benefit; the great majority preferred not to do so or had no preference either way;

- landlords and agents who preferred not to let to people on Housing Benefit gave as their reasons the administration of the scheme, the precarious financial position of such tenants, and the perceived 'undesirability' of benefit recipients;

- nearly two fifths of addresses had landlords or agents who said they had experience of Rent Officer referrals;

- among those who had experience of Rent Officer referrals, there was, very approximately, an even split between addresses where the landlord or agent said the rent had never been restricted and those where they said it had been restricted on at least one occasion;

- a minority of landlords (31% of the all lettings sample and 23% of the recent lettings sample) said that, in setting the rent for their accommodation, they always or sometimes took into account the fact that the rent might be referred to the Rent Officer for Housing Benefit purposes;

- landlords and agents of over three quarters of addresses disagreed with the view that landlords could charge tenants on Housing Benefit a higher rent;

Introduction

8.1 Housing Benefit is an income related social security payment administered by local authorities on behalf of the Department of Social Security. According to the Survey of English Housing, just over a third (36%) of private tenants were in receipt of Housing Benefit in 1993/94 (Carey, 1995). It thus plays an important role in the privately rented sector. This chapter therefore examines landlords' and agents' knowledge and experience of letting to tenants who are in receipt of Housing Benefit. In particular, it looks at whether landlords and agents had heard of Housing Benefit and/or let their accommodation to tenants who were receiving it; landlords' and agents' letting preferences in respect of Housing Benefit and whether they thought it was possible to charge recipients a higher rent than those not receiving benefit; their experience of Rent Officer referrals for Housing Benefit purposes and whether they took this into account in setting the rent for their accommodation.

Knowledge and experience of Housing Benefit

8.2 The great majority of private landlords and agents had heard of Housing Benefit. The owners (or agents) of 95% of all lettings and 97% of recent lettings had heard about the scheme. Asked whether any of their current tenants were receiving Housing Benefit, the owners and agents of 72% and 69% of lettings respectively said that they had; 5% and 3% said they did not know, and the remainder (23% and 29%) said they had no current tenants receiving it (Table 8.1).

Table 8.1 : Whether any of the landlords' (or their agents') current tenants were on Housing Benefit	All lettings	Most recent lettings
	%	%
At least 1 on HB	72	69
None on HB	23	29
Don't know	5	3
Total	**100**	**100**
(Base)	(286)	(496)

Base: addresses where landlords and agents had heard of HB

8.3 Table 8.2 shows both the mean weekly rent for the most recent letting at the address, and the estimated vacant possession value of the address, by whether or not the landlord (or agent) said at least one of the tenants in their portfolio (not necessarily the sampled address) was receiving Housing Benefit.

8.4 The mean weekly rent where the landlord or agent said that they were letting at least one of the properties to someone on Housing Benefit was lower in both samples than where they said they were not letting to anyone on Housing Benefit. In the all lettings sample, the mean rent was £63 where the landlord or agent said that at least one of their properties was let to a Housing Benefit recipient, compared with £94 where they were not; in the recent lettings sample, the corresponding figures were £80 and £100 respectively (Table 8.2).

8.5 This pattern was repeated for the mean estimated vacant possession value of the address. Thus, in both samples, the estimated vacant possession value of the address was much lower where the landlord or agent said that at least one of their tenants was on Housing Benefit than where they said that none were receiving it: £63 thousand compared with £77 thousand in the all lettings sample, and £83 thousand compared with £130 thousand in the recent lettings sample (Table 8.2).

Table 8.2 : Average weekly rent for the most recent letting and estimated vacant possession value of the address by whether or not at least one of the landlord (or agent's) tenants was on Housing Benefit

	Weekly rent		Vacant possession values	
	All lettings	Recent lettings	All lettings	Recent lettings
At least 1 tenant on HB	£63	£80	£63,384	£83,155
None on HB	£94	£100	£76,509	£130,013
(Base)	(137)	(450)	(241)	(409)

8.6   Landlords and agents who said they were not currently letting to any tenants on Housing Benefit were asked if they had ever done so. Most of the landlords and agents who thought they were not letting to Housing Benefit recipients said that they had never done so: this was the case for the respondents at six out of 10 addresses in the all lettings sample and seven out of 10 in the recent lettings sample who were not currently letting to such tenants (Table 8.3).

8.7   It is important to note, however, that landlords' knowledge about whether or not a tenant of theirs is on Housing Benefit may be inaccurate. It is tenants who are eligible to apply for Housing Benefit and they who are entitled to receive it (though of course in some cases the payment is made directly to the landlord). Hence it is possible that some landlords who believe that they are not letting their accommodation to people on Housing Benefit may, in fact, be doing so. A survey of private landlords in Scotland found that one in seven addresses where the landlord (or agent) said they had never let accommodation to tenants on Housing Benefit, had in fact been occupied by a recipient in the year before the interviews were carried out (Kemp and Rhodes, 1994).

Table 8.3 : Whether landlords (or their agents) who were not currently letting to tenants on Housing Benefit had ever done so

	All lettings	Most recent lettings
	%	%
Had let to tenants on HB	25	28
Had never let to tenants on HB	60	69
Don't know	15	4
Total	**100**	**100**
(Base)	(79)	(153)

Base: addresses where landlords and agents had heard of HB but were not currently letting to recipients

Housing Benefit and letting preferences

8.8   In recent years there has been much controversy over whether or not private landlords prefer to let to tenants on Housing Benefit or prefer to avoid them. Landlords and agents were therefore asked for their preferences in this respect. In fact, only about one in 20 addresses in both samples had a landlord or agent who said that they preferred to let to tenants who were on Housing Benefit. This figure is very similar to that found in a survey of private landlords in Scotland carried out in 1993 (Kemp and Rhodes, 1994). The owners or agents of just over half of the addresses in both samples said that they preferred to let to tenants who were *not* receiving Housing Benefit, while about four out of 10 said they had no preference either way (Table 8.4).

8.9   Thus while the majority of landlords and agents were currently letting to tenants on Housing Benefit, many would actually prefer not to be doing so. None of the respondents at addresses owned by institutional landlords said they preferred to let to tenants on Housing Benefit and they were much more likely, compared with other types of landlord, to say they had no preference (Table 8.5).

Table 8.4 : Whether, in general, landlords or their agents prefer to let to tenants on Housing Benefit

	All lettings	Most recent lettings
	%	%
Prefers tenants on HB	6	5
Prefers tenants not on HB	53	55
No preference	52	40
Total	**100**	**100**
(Base)	(282)	(485)

Base: addresses where landlords and agents had heard of HB

Table 8.5 : Whether, in general, the landlord prefers to let to tenants on Housing Benefit by type of landlord

	All letting			Recent lettings		
	Business	Sideline	Institu-tional	Business	Sideline	Institu-tional
	%	%	%	%	%	%
Prefers tenants on HB	2	8	-	6	6	-
Prefers tenants not on HB	46	56	36	62	57	31
No preference	52	36	64	32	38	69
Total	**100**	**100**	**100**	**100**	**100**	**100**
(Base)	(52)	(205)	(25)	(82)	(359)	(42)

Base: addresses where landlords and agents had heard of HB

8.10 The reasons why landlords and agents preferred not to let to tenants on Housing Benefit are shown in Table 8.6. The results are expressed as a percentage of lettings where landlords and agents said they preferred not to let to people on Housing Benefit. The reasons given by landlords and agents can be grouped into those that were to do with the administration of the scheme, the perceived image that they have of Housing Benefit recipients, the financially weak position of tenants on benefit, and a miscellany of other factors.

Table 8.6 : Reasons why landlords or their agents preferred not to let to people on Housing Benefit

	All lettings	Most recent lettings
	%	%
Administration reasons		
Long initial delays in getting HB	21	25
Recovery of overpaid HB	18	18
Problems caused by HB not being paid direct to landlord	18	14
Red tape/bureaucracy	10	9
HB payment cycle	12	5
Lack of information about HB	1	9
Claimant reasons		
Tenants on HB are financially insecure	32	21
HB tenants are undesirable	27	36
Tenants on HB would not be able to afford the rent	7	6
Can't get deposits from HB tenants	2	4
Other reasons		
HB rent restrictions	14	10
More difficult to regain possession	7	5
Problems getting insurance cover	6	3
Other reasons	6	10
(Base)	(148)	(268)

Base: addresses where landlords and agents preferred not to let to tenants on HB

8.11 Among respondents who preferred not to let to tenants on Housing Benefit, 21% in the all lettings sample and 13% in the recent lettings sample said that long initial delays in the processing of claims was a reason why they preferred not to let to tenants on Housing Benefit. Eighteen % in both samples mentioned the recovery of over paid benefit from the landlord when Housing Benefit is paid direct. This can occur where tenants' circumstances have changed and they have failed to notify the local authority either at all or in sufficient time; landlords sometimes find it difficult to reclaim the excess Housing Benefit from the tenant, especially if they have moved on to other accommodation. Fourteen % and 10% respectively of respondents in the two samples said they preferred not to let to tenants on Housing Benefit because of the eligible rent being restricted.

8.12 A subtantial minority of landlords and agents who preferred not to let to claimants - 27% in the all lettings sample and 36% in the recent lettings sample - stated that tenants on Housing Benefit were 'undesirable'. Claimants were viewed in this light either because they were thought to take less care of the property, because they were perceived to be less reliable financially, or were felt to be in some other way less attractive as tenants than people who were not on Housing Benefit. Respondents at 32% of addresses in the all lettings sample where the landlord or agent preferred not to let to people on Housing Benefit and 21% in the recent lettings sample, said that it was because they were financially less secure than tenants who were in work. Despite the publicity which the issue has received in the national press, only 6% and 3% of those who preferred not to let to claimants in each of the two respective samples said that it was because letting to tenants on Housing Benefit made it difficult for them to get insurance cover on the property.

Rent Officer referrals and rent setting

8.13 When private tenants whose tenancy commenced after 14 January 1989 apply for Housing Benefit, their rent and accommodation details are referred to the Rent Officer Service. At the time of the survey, Rent Officers were required to apply a number of tests of reasonableness. First, they had to determine whether or not the rent was significantly above a reasonable market level; and, if it was, to determine what would be a reasonable market rent for the accommodation. Second, they had to determine whether the accommodation was over-large for the claimant's needs according to specified accommodation size criteria; and, if it was over-large, to determine a notional market rent for the accommodation assuming that it was not over-large. Third, they had to determine whether the rent, even if it was not over the market value or over-large, was nevertheless 'exceptionally high'; and, if it was, to determine the 'highest reasonable rent' which would not be exceptionally high[†].

8.14 At the time of the survey, the purpose of these referrals was to determine thresholds on the amount of rent which would be eligible for subsidy from central government in respect of Housing Benefit payments made by the local authority. Local authorities had quite separately to make decisions about the reasonableness of the rent and of the accommodation in each individual case. However, a survey of local authority Housing Benefit services found that, in the great majority of cases, local authorities used the Rent Officer's determination as the eligible rent for Housing Benefit purposes (Kemp and McLaverty, 1994).

8.15 The Rent Officer referral process and the rules governing the eligible rent for Housing Benefit purposes were substantially modified in January 1996, after the survey of private landlords was carried out (see Zebedee and Ward, 1995 for details). Further changes are proposed for implementation in October 1996.

---

† This is intended only as a brief summary of the Rent Officer referral arrangements. Fuller detail is provided by Zebedee and Ward (1995) and Findlay et al (1995). See also Kemp and McLaverty (1993).

8.16 Respondents who had heard of Housing Benefit were asked whether any of their tenants had ever had their rent referred to the Rent Officer by the local authority's Housing Benefit service. It should be stressed that the responses to this question are about landlord and agent perceptions and knowledge. Recent qualitative research on private landlords found that many of them, especially sideline landlords, were unaware of the Rent Officer service or their involvement in the Housing Benefit scheme (Bevan *et al.*, 1995). Thus the figures are likely to under estimate the true extent to which the respondents' tenants had had their rent referred to the Rent Officer.

8.17 In both samples, nearly two fifths of addresses had landlords and agents who said that at least one of their tenants had had their rent referred to the Rent Officer for Housing Benefit purposes. Just over half had landlords or agents who said that none had been referred to the Rent Officer in this way (Table 8.7). Across both samples, there was a broadly similar pattern of difference between landlord types in response to this question. Respondents at addresses with business landlords were more likely than the average to say they had had tenants whose rent had been referred to the rent officer, while institutional landlords were less likely than the average to report this. The experiences of sideline landlords were similar to the results for landlords as a whole, but when disagregated differences existed between investment and noninvestment motivated sideline landlords (Table 8.8). In both samples, respondents at 39% of investor sideline addresses compared with 24% at noninvestor sideline addresses, said that they had tenants whose rent had been referred to the rent officer.

Table 8.7 : Whether any of the landlords' or their agents' tenants had had their rent referred to the Rent Officer by the local authority Housing Benefit Service

	All lettings	Most recent lettings
	%	%
Yes	38	38
No	56	53
Don't know	7	9
Total	**100**	**100**
(Base)	(285)	(489)

Base: addresses where landlords and agents had heard of HB

Table 8.8 : Whether any of the landlords' or their agents' tenants had had their rent referred to the Rent Officer by the local authority Housing Benefit Service, by type of landlord

	All lettings			Recent lettings		
	Business	Sideline	Institu-tional	Business	Sideline	Institu-tional
	%	%	%	%	%	%
Yes	52	37	18	54	37	16
No	35	58	82	37	55	68
Don't know	14	6	-	11	8	16
Total	**100**	**100**	**100**	**100**	**100**	**100**
(Base)	(52)	(205)	(28)	(82)	(361)	(44)

Base: addresses where landlords and agents had heard of HB

8.18 Where the landlord or agent said that they had had tenants whose rent had been referred to the Rent Officer for Housing Benefit purposes, they were asked whether the rent had always been accepted or had ever been restricted. As Table 8.9 shows, there was, very approximately, an even split between those who said it had always been accepted and those who said it had been restricted on at least one occasion. In all lettings sample, 47% said that the rent has always been accepted and 45% that it had been restricted at least once; while in the recent lettings sample, the figures were 45% and 50% respectively. Five % in the all lettings sample and 2% in the recent lettings sample said they did not know whether the rent had ever been restricted.

Table 8.9 : Whether any of the landlords' or their agents' tenants had ever had their rent restricted for Housing Benefit by the Rent Officer

	All lettings	Most recent lettings
	%	%
Rent always accepted	47	45
Rent has been restricted	45	50
Agree rent with the Rent Officer	4	2
Don't know	5	2
Total	**100**	**100**
(Base)	(107)	(185)

Base: addresses where landlords and agents had heard of HB and had tenants whose rent had been referred to the Rent Officer

8.19 A very small number of landlords said that they agreed the rent with the Rent Officer and therefore, by implication, that it was not a case of the rent being either restricted or not restricted. This raises the question of whether, in setting the rent, landlords and agents more generally are influenced by the Rent Officers' role in Housing Benefit. Respondents who had heard of Housing Benefit were therefore asked whether they always, sometimes or never took the Rent Officer into account when setting the rent.

8.20 As Table 8.10 shows, landlords and agents at 21% of addresses in the all lettings sample and 14% in the recent lettings sample, said that they *always* took the role of the Rent Officer into account when setting the rent for their accommodation; a further 10% and 9% respectively said that they *sometimes* did so. Landlords and agents at the majority of addresses - 65% and 72% respectively - said that they *never* took the Rent Officer into account.

Table 8.10 : Whether landlords or their agents take into account what the Rent Officer will accept for Housing Benefit when setting the rent

	All lettings	Most recent lettings
	%	%
Always takes Rent Officer into account	21	14
Sometimes takes Rent Officer into account	10	9
Never takes Rent Officer into account	65	72
Not applicable	4	5
Total	**100**	**100**
(Base)	(273)	(479)
Base: addresses landlords and agents had heard of HB		

Table 8.11 : Whether landlords or their agents agreed or disagreed with the statement that 'Landlords can charge a higher rent to tenants on Housing Benefit'

	All lettings	Most recent lettings
	%	%
Strongly agree	-	1
Agree	9	11
Neither agree nor disagree	9	10
Disagree	49	44
Disagree strongly	12	9
Can't say	22	24
Total	**100**	**100**
(Base)	(298)	(509)

Base: all addresses

8.21 Finally, respondents were asked whether they agreed or disagreed with the statement that *Landlords can charge a higher rent to tenants on Housing Benefit*. In both samples, the respondents at the majority of addresses disagreed with this statement. In the all lettings sample, 61% disagreed and in the recent lettings sample 53% said the same. Twenty-two % and 24% of addresses respectively in the two samples had owners or agents who said that they could not say one way or the other whether landlords could charge a higher rent or not to Housing Benefit recipients. A further 9% and 10% respectively they neither agreed nor disagreed with the statement. Amongst those who felt able to express an opinion, the number of addresses where the respondent disagreed with the statement was greatly in excess of those who agreed with it, especially among the all lettings sample. Nevertheless, landlords and agents responsible for 9% of addresses in the all lettings sample and 12% in the recent lettings sample, agreed that it was possible to charge a higher rent to tenants on Housing Benefit (Table 8.11).

9   The legislative framework

Summary   The main findings of this chapter are that:

- a significant minority of lettings have landlords who did not know what types of agreement they used when letting accommodation;

- one in five lettings had landlords who had let on assured tenancies and six in 10 had landlords who had let on assured shorthold tenancies;

- the most often mentioned advantages of assured and assured shorthold tenancies related to the ability of landlords to regain possession and to greater flexibility in general;

- the most often mentioned disadvantage of assured tenancies was the difficulty experienced in regaining possession;

- over half landlords with assured shorthold tenancies said they had no disadvantages.

- half landlords thought the situation had changed to their advantage since 1988; only a quarter said it had changed to their disadvantage: those that did referred to the greater completion between landlords.

Introduction   9.1   The Housing Act, 1988 established a new framework for letting. It enabled landlords to let new lettings at market rents and with contractual security. The intention was to give landlords the confidence that they could let at market rents without tenants being able to refer rents for determination to a third party (except in limited circumstances). It was also intended to create greater and more predictable liquidity for landlords' investments, by giving them more confidence and certainty about the timing and circumstances under which they could get repossession of their properties.

9.2   In particular it enabled landlords to choose between two types of agreement when letting new tenancies for accommodation which is available to the general public. First, assured tenancies, let at market rents, but with security for tenants. Second, assured shorthold tenancies, also let at market rents, but with no security for tenants beyond a fixed term, which can be for as little as six months. Other changes were made to the legal framework which enabled landlords to seek repossession of lettings because, for example, tenants were in arrears with rents, by altering the mandatory and discretionary grounds for the courts to grant possession orders to landlords seeking to evict tenants.

9.3   The objectives of this Chapter are to:

- examine the types of letting agreements that landlords and agents have used in the past;

- look at the advantages and disadvantages of assured tenancies and assured shorthold tenancies identified by those landlords and agents who have had experience of these agreements;

- analyse whether the advantages and disadvantages identified were related in any way to different landlord types;

- whether landlords believed that the situation had changed to their advantage since 1988.

9.4   The findings in this Chapter, unlike the preceding ones, are not related to the two specific samples (of all lettings and of recent lettings), but to the landlords' and agents' experience and views in general. The landlords and agents interviewed were the owners and managers of a representative sample of all lettings in England. There is thus no distinction in the Tables between the two letting samples.

Types of letting agreements used

9.5   Landlords and agents were asked if they had ever let on a recognised type of letting agreement at any of their tenancies. They were shown a card listing these. The list is the one shown on Table 9.5.

9.6   Almost all the lettings through agents had managers who had used one or more of these types of agreements. Very few had used any other type (Table 9.1).

Table 9.1 : Proportion of lettings whose landlords and agents had used recognised types of letting agreement		
	Landlord	Agent
	%	%
Used	83	98
Don't know	2	-
Not used	14	2
Base	543	270
Base: all lettings		

9.7   However, 16% of lettings had landlords who either did not know what types of agreement they had used or who said that they had not used any one of those on the list (Table 9.1). Given that landlords were asked to select from a list containing all types of recognised letting agreements, this reinforces other findings (for example in Chapter 6) showing that a significant minority of lettings had landlords who were unaware of the legislative framework within which they could make letting agreements with their tenants.

Table 9.2 : Proportion of lettings whose landlords had used recognised lettings agreements by size of landlords' total lettings portfolio

| | Total number of lettings | | | | |
	1	2-7	8-40	41+	All
	%	%	%	%	%
Used	66	82	93	93	83
Don't know	5	2	1	1	2
Not used	29	16	6	6	14
Base	138	132	123	150	543

Base: all lettings when landlord interviewed

Table 9.3 : Proportion of lettings whose landlords had used recognised lettings agreements by type of landlords

| | Type of landlord | | | | |
| | Sideline sample letting | | Business | Institutional | All |
	Not investment	Investment			
	%	%	%	%	%
Used	75	87	89	90	83
Don't know	4	2	-	2	2
No	21	11	11	8	14
Base	197	184	103	59	543

Base: all lettings where landlord interviewed

Table 9.4 : Proportion of lettings whose landlord had used recognised types of lettings agreements by 'old' and 'new' landlords

	'Old' landlords	'New' landlords
	%	%
Used	85	76
Don't know	2	4
No	13	19
Base	377	199

Base: all lettings where landlord interviewed

9.8   This lack of awareness was greater amongst some types of landlords than others:

- landlords with smaller portfolios were more likely than those with larger ones not to know what types of agreement they had used (Table 9.2);

- sideline landlords (for whom their sample letting was not an investment) were more likely not to know than other sideline landlords and business and institutional landlords (Table 9.3);

- new landlords (that is those who had acquired all their lettings in England on or since deregulation in 1989) were also more likely not to know what agreements they had used than landlords who had acquired some or all of their lettings before deregulation (Table 9.4).

Table 9.5 : Types of agreement used by landlords and agents

Types of agreement	Proportion of lettings whose landlords or agents have used agreement	
	Landlord	Agent
Assured shorthold tenancy	60%	94%
Regulated (Rent Act) tenancy	26%	56%
Accommodation tied to job	22%	21%
Assured tenancy	18%	63%
Shorthold (1980 Act) tenancy	16%	36%
Holiday let (in season)	6%	10%
Company let	6%	46%
Holiday let (off season)	4%	14%
Nonexecutive occupancy licence	3%	7%

Accommodation with meals and laundry	3%	3%
Some other	10%	11%
Can't say	<1%	-
Base	543	270

9.9   Table 9.5 shows what proportion of lettings had landlords or managers who had ever let on each of the types of agreement listed in the Table.

9.10 Only 18% of lettings had landlords who had let on assured tenancies (i.e. assured tenancies that are not assured shorthold tenancies), although nearly two thirds, (63%), of lettings with agents had managers who had let in this way in the past (indeed, not unexpectedly, agents had a much greater experience of all the types of letting agreements listed than did landlords).

Table 9.6 : Types of agreement used by landlords by size of landlords' total lettings portfolio

Types of agreement	Total number of lettings				
	1	2-7	8-40	41+	All
Assured shorthold tenancy	45%	52%	70%	70%	60%
Regulated (Rent Act) tenancy	6%	15%	27%	54%	26%
Accommodation tied to job	1%	12%	22%	51%	22%
Assured tenancy	4%	7%	19%	41%	18%
Shorthold (1980 Act) tenancy	9%	14%	19%	20%	16%
Holiday let (in season)	2%	5%	9%	7%	6%
Company let	1%	4%	4%	15%	6%
Holiday let (off season)	1%	3%	4%	6%	4%
Nonexecutive occupancy licence	-	2%	1%	8%	3%
Accommodation with meals and laundry	1%	2%	5%	6%	3%
Some other	5%	8%	15%	13%	10%
Can't say	-	1%	-	-	<1%
Base	138	132	123	150	543

Base: all lettings where landlord interviewed

Table 9.7 : Types of agreement used by landlords by landlord type

| | Landlord type | | | | |
| | Sideline sample letting | | Business | Institu-tional | All |
	Non-invest-ment	Invest-ment			
Assured shorthold tenancy	50%	65%	75%	52%	60%
Regulated (Rent Act) tenancy	15%	24%	48%	30%	26%
Accommodation tied to job	25%	12%	15%	5%	22%
Assured tenancy	13%	11%	33%	32%	18%
Shorthold (1980 Act) tenancy	12%	18%	23%	7%	16%
Holiday let (in season)	4%	8%	6%	7%	6%
Company let	5%	6%	10%	5%	6%
Holiday let (off season)	1%	6%	3%	36%	4%
Nonexecutive occupancy licence	3%	3%	1%	7%	3%
Accommodation with meals and laundry	4%	2%	3%	7%	3%
Some other	10%	9%	9%	17%	10%
Can't say	-	1%	-	-	<1%
Base	197	184	103	59	543

Base: all lettings where landlord interviewed

Table 9.8 : Types of agreement used by 'old' and 'new' landlords

| Types of agreement | Percentage of lettings owned by | |
	'Old' landlords	'New' landlords
Assured shorthold tenancy	58%	61%
Regulated (Rent Act) tenancy	30%	7%
Accommodation tied to job	23%	5%
Assured tenancy	19%	7%
Shorthold (1980 Act) tenancy	18%	8%
Holiday let (in season)	7%	3%
Company let	7%	2%
Holiday let (off season)	4%	2%
Nonexecutive occupancy licence	3%	1%

Accommodation with meals and laundry	4%	2%
Some other	11%	6%
Can't say	<1%	<1%
Base	377	119

Base: all lettings where landlords interviewed

9.11 Amongst landlords:

- landlords with larger portfolios were more likely to have let on assured tenancies than those with smaller ones: for example 41% of lettings with the largest landlords had owners who had let in this way, compared with only 7% of lettings whose landlords owned between two and seven lettings throughout England (Table 9.6);

- business and institutional landlords were more likely to have let on assured tenancies than sideline landlords (Table 9.7);

- new landlords were much less likely to have let on assured tenancies than more long-standing, or 'old' landlords (Table 9.8).

9.12 As Table 9.5 also shows, there was much greater use of assured shorthold tenancies than of assured tenancies. Indeed 94% of lettings with agents had managers who had let on this agreement. Moreover 60% of lettings had landlords who had let in this way.

9.13 Amongst landlords:

- landlords with larger portfolios were more likely than those with smaller ones to have let on assured shorthold tenancies (Table 9.6);

- business landlords were more likely to have let this way than others, especially institutional and sideline landlords (whose sample letting was not regarded as an investment) (Table 9.7);

- new and long-standing landlords were equally likely to have used assured shortholds (Table 9.8).

9.14 As many as 36% of agents had let on shorthold tenancies created under the 1980 Housing Act and 16% of lettings had landlords who had also done so (Table 9.5). Again, as expected, landlords with larger portfolios, business landlords, and sideline landlords whose sample letting was an investment had let on 1980 Act shortholds (Tables 9.6 and 9.7.). Noteworthy is the fact that 8% of the lettings owned by new landlords said they had let in this way, despite the fact that such lettings could not be created after 1988: a further indication of landlords' uncertainty and lack of knowledge about the types of letting agreement they could use (unless of course these were lettings that such landlords had acquired with sitting tenants since 1988) (Table 9.8).

9.15 Over half the lettings with agents had managers who had let on regulated tenancies. Over a quarter of lettings had landlords who had let in this way (Table 9.5). It was landlords with larger portfolios, business, and 'old' , long-standing landlords who had let such tenancies (Tables 9.6, 9.7 and 9.8). Again, it should be noted that 7% of lettings with new landlords had owners who said they had let in this way, although no such tenancies can have been created since 1988. Of course, it is possible that some or all of these lettings were acquired with sitting tenants since 1988, or, alternatively, that these 'new' landlords were in fact owners who had owned dwellings before 1989 but had sold all of them subsequently (Table 9.8).

9.16 As Table 9.5 shows, with the exception of agreements related to accommodation which went with employment, all the other types of agreement listed had been used by only a small minority of landlords.

9.17 Approximately one in five of lettings were tied to a job. These agreements were either licences or tenancies and, if they had been the latter, it would have technically been assured tenancies, with a ground for possession if employment ceased.

9.18 Tied accommodation agreements had been used much more by landlords with larger than with smaller portfolios. Indeed, they had been used by the owners of half the lettings which were part of the largest portfolios (Table 9.6). Whilst they were also more likely to have been used by institutional than by other types of landlords, a quarter of lettings owned by sideline landlords for noninvestment purposes had owners who had let on tied accommodation agreements (Table 9.7). Nearly a quarter of the lettings with older landlords had owners who had let in this way compared with only 5% of those owned by new landlords (Table 9.8).

9.20 Amongst the other types of letting agreement, it was only company lets and those where meals and laundry were provided where there were differences in use by different types of landlord. Company lets were used far more by landlords with larger portfolios and by older more long-standing landlords, than others (Tables 9.6 and 9.8). Agreements which provided meals and laundry had been used more by landlords with larger portfolios (Table 9.6).

9.21 Not unexpectedly, agents had more experience of using these 'minority' agreements than landlords (Table 9.5). Nearly half the lettings with managing agents had managers who had used company lets and 14% had let holiday accommodation out of season, both forms of letting agreements that provided limited security to those to whom it was let.

Assured Tenancies: advantages

9.22 Those who had let on assured tenancies (Table 9.5) were asked to say what they thought were the advantages and disadvantages of letting in this way, compared with other types of letting.

Table 9.9 : Advantages of assured tenancies mentioned by landlords agents		
Advantages	Landlords	Agents
No advantages	28%	36%
Can charge market rent/can set own rent level/can charge higher rent	18%	17%
Landlords can regain possession/get rid of unreasonable tenants	16%	18%
Generally feel more in control/greater flexibility/easier to manage property	15%	2%
Tenants get security of tenure/do not have to leave property at end of lease	8%	9%
No minimum length tenancy/can arrange longer-term lets/do not have to renew lease	7%	6%
Flexibility of being able to arrange short lets (of < 6 months)	2%	11%
Greater opportunity to increase rent levels	2%	3%
Other	6%	11%
Vague/irrelevant/unspecific	7%	3%
Don't know	4%	3%
Not answered	2%	-
Base	100	170
Base: all lettings whose landlords or agents had let on assured tenancies		

9.23 As Table 9.9 shows, 28% of lettings whose landlords had let in this way had owners who said that it had no advantages. Furthermore the agents of 36% of lettings also said there were no advantages. There were no significant differences amongst landlords of different portfolio sizes and types in the proportions who thought there were no advantages (Tables 9.10 and 9.11). However, those who said that assured tenancies had no advantages were more likely to have said that they had a problem letting accommodation since 1988, either when deciding upon the types of letting agreement to use, renewing them, ending them or regaining possession (see Chapter 11 below). For example, 47% of those landlords who thought there were no advantages to assured tenancies had a problem ending agreements since 1988, compared with only 27% of those who thought there were advantages.

Table 9.10 : Advantages of assured tenancies by size of landlords' total lettings portfolio

Advantages	Total number of lettings				
	1	2-7	8-40	41+	All
No advantages	17%	22%	47%	23%	28%
Can charge market rent/can set own rent level/can charge higher rent	-	-	-	29%	18%
Landlords can regain possession/get rid of unreasonable tenants	-	33%	22%	13%	16%
Generally feel more in control/greater flexibility/easier to manage property	17%	11%	17%	14%	15%
Tenants get security of tenure/do not have to leave property at end of lease	-	-	4%	11%	8%
No minimum length tenancy/can arrange longer-term lets/do not have to renew lease	-	-	-	11%	7%
Flexibility of being able to arrange short lets (of < 6 months)	-	-	-	3%	2%
Greater opportunity to increase rent levels	-	-	-	3%	2%
Other	-	-	9%	6%	6%
Vague/irrelevant/unspecific	17%	22%	4%	5%	7%
Don't know	33%	11%	-	2%	4%
Not answered	17%	-	-	2%	2%
Base	6	9	23	62	100

Base: all lettings whose landlords had let on assured tenancies

120

Advantages	Landlord type				
	Sideline sample letting		Business	Institu-tion	All
	Non-invest-ment	Invest-ment			
No advantages	31%	14%	41%	16%	28%
Can charge market rent/can set own rent level/can charge higher rent	11%	-	32%	21%	18%
Landlords can regain possession/get rid of unreasonable tenants	8%	33%	15%	10%	16%
Generally feel more in control/greater flexibility/ easier to manage property	15%	19%	3%	32%	15%
Tenants get security of tenure/do not have to leave property at end of lease	11%	14%	3%	5%	8%
No minimum length tenancy/can arrange longer-term lets/do not have to renew lease	11%	5%	6%	5%	7%
Flexibility of being able to arrange short lets (of <6 months)	-	-	3%	5%	2%
Greater opportunity to increase rent levels	-	5%	-	5%	2%
Other	-	9%	9%	5%	6%
Vague/irrelevant/unspecific	15%	9%	3%	-	7%
Don't know	4%	9%	-	5%	4%
Not answered	4%	-	-	5%	2%
Base	26	21	34	19	100

Table 9.11 : Advantages of assured tenancies by type of landlord

Base: all lettings whose landlords let on assured tenancies

9.24 The advantages cited for assured tenancies fell into a number of groups, although most of them related to issues concerned with security of tenure and control than to rent levels (Table 9.9).

9.25 However, about one in five landlords and agents mentioned either the fact that market rents could be charged or that there was a greater opportunity to increase rent levels. These advantages were particularly held by landlords with larger portfolios and by business and institutional than by other landlords (Tables 9.10 and 9.11).

9.26 Approximately the same proportion of landlords and agents, 16% and 18% respectively, mentioned the ability to regain possession and to 'get rid' of unreasonable tenants (Table 9.9). Whilst this was mentioned as an advantage more often by landlords with smaller portfolios than by those with larger ones and also more by sideline landlords regarding their sample letting as an investment than by others, these were not statistically significant differences (Tables 9.10 and 9.11). Thus, whilst there is some evidence of a 'portfolio effect' (that is, smaller landlords being less able to diversify risk and therefore benefiting proportionately more than larger ones from this attribute), it is not a pronounced one. This is the case for all types of landlords.

9.27 The other advantages mentioned were connected to the greater flexibility and control assured tenancies afforded to landlords and agents, compared with other types of letting agreement (Table 9.9).

9.28 These included the ability to create short term lets of less than six months, which over 11% agents cited, although only 2% of lettings had landlords mentioning this (it should be noted however that, unless a specific ground can be proved, the tenancy cannot be ended at the end of a short term - see Appendix).

9.29 Approximately the same proportion of lettings had landlords and agents (7% and 6% respectively) who said that assured tenancies allowed them to create longer term lettings.

9.30 Fifteen % of lettings had landlords who mentioned factors related to the greater control or flexibility they had in managing lettings, although only a small proportion (2%) of agents noted this.

9.31 Nearly 1 in 10 of lettings had landlords and agents who identified the security of tenure that tenants had as one of the advantages of assured tenancies.

9.32 Finally, it is important to note that some landlords and agents were uncertain about what the advantages were. These uncertainties were mentioned more by those with smaller portfolios and by sideline landlords than by others (Tables 9.10 and 9.11).

Assured tenancies: disadvantages

9.33 Whilst both landlords and agents with experience of letting assured tenancies identified disadvantages, the landlords of 39% of lettings and the agents of 21% of lettings said there were no disadvantages (Table 9.12). Approximately the same proportions of landlords with different sized portfolios and of different types thought there were no disadvantages (Tables 9.13 and 9.14). Those who said there were no disadvantages were more likely not to have had problems letting accommodation since 1988.

Table 9.12 : Disadvantages of assured tenancies mentioned by landlords and agents		
Disadvantages of assured tenancies	Landlords	Agents
Difficulty in gaining (vacant) possession at end of lease/lack of flexibility for landlord because of this/difficulty to see	48%	66%
No disadvantages	39%	21%
Rents too low/rent officers can restrict rent	4%	3%
Problems related to drawing up agreement	2%	2%
Other	3%	8%
Vague/irrelevant/unspecific	2%	2%
Don't know	5%	3%
Not answered	2%	-
Base	100	170

Base: all lettings whose landlords or agents let on assured tenancies

9.33 One disadvantage dominated those mentioned by both landlords and agents. This was the difficulty they experienced in getting vacant possession. Nearly half the lettings with landlords who had let on assured tenancies had owners who said this. All types and portfolio sizes of landlords said so in about the same proportions. So too did the agents of two thirds of the lettings (Table 9.12).

9.34 A few landlords and agents mentioned a number of other disadvantages, such as rents being too low or being restricted by rent officers (sic) and problems experienced drawing up agreements.

Table 9.13 : Disadvantages of assured tenancies by size of landlords' total lettings portfolio

Disadvantages of assured tenancies	Total number of lettings				
	1	2-7	8-40	41+	All
Difficulty in gaining (vacant) possession at end of lease/lack of flexibility for landlord because of this/difficult to sell	-	44%	52%	52%	48%
No disadvantages	50%	44%	39%	37%	39%
Rents too low/rent officers can restrict rent	-	11%	-	5%	4%
Problems related to drawing up agreement	-	-	4%	2%	2%
Other	-	-	4%	3%	3%
Vague/irrelevant/unspecific	-	-	4%	2%	2%
Don't know	33%	11%	-	3%	5%
Not answered	17%	-	-	2%	2%
Base	6	9	23	62	100

Base: all landlords who let on assured tenancies

Table 9.14 : Disadvantages of assured tenancies by type of landlord

Disadvantages of assured tenancies	Landlord type				
	Sideline sample letting		Busi-ness	Institu-tion	All
	Non-invest-ment	Invest-ment			
Difficulty in gaining (vacant possession at end of lease/lack of flexibility for landlord because of this/difficult to sell	46%	57%	53%	32%	48%
No disadvantages	35%	29%	41%	53%	39%
Rents too low/rent officers can restrict rent	8%	9%	-	-	4%
Problems related to drawing up agreement	4%	4%	-	-	2%
Other	-	5%	3%	5%	3%
Vague/irrelevant/unspecific	4%	-	-	5%	2%
Don't know	4%	9%	3%	5%	5%
Not answered	8%	-	-	-	2%
Base	26	21	34	19	100

Base: all lettings whose landlords let on assured tenancies

Assured shorthold tenancies: advantages

9.34 As Table 9.5 showed, a much greater proportion of landlords and agents had experience of letting on assured shorthold tenancies than of assured tenancies. Their views on the advantages of assured shortholds are listed in Table 9.15.

Table 9.15 : Advantage of assured shorthold tenancies		
Advantages	Landlords	Agents
Easier/guaranteed repossession at end of lease	80%	82%
Fixed term tenancies - can review situation at end of lease	11%	18%
Can charge market rents/can set own rent level	9%	19%
Greater mutual awareness of rights	8%	17%
Generally feel more in control/greater flexibility/easier to manage property	7%	5%
No advantages	3%	1%
Other	1%	7%
Vague/irrelevant/unspecific	2%	<1%
Don't know	1%	1%
Not answered	2%	2%
Base	325	255

Base: all lettings whose landlords or agents let on assured shorthold tenancies

9.35 It should be noted that only a small proportion said there were no advantages at all, compared to other types of letting, and that most of the advantages cited related to getting possession and to having more flexibility, than to the ability to charge market rents.

9.36 Eighty % of lettings had landlords and 82% had agents who mentioned the ease of getting possession at the end of a tenancy as one of the advantages. This view was held by as large a proportion of landlords whatever their portfolio size and type and whether they were a 'new' or 'old' (long-standing) landlord (Tables 9.16 to 9.18). Moreover, the landlords of 11% of lettings and the agents of 18% of the lettings noted the related point that, because assured shorthold tenancies were for a fixed term, they were able to review the situation at the end of the lease (an advantage cited more by larger portfolio than smaller landlords - Table 9.16).

Table 9.16 : Advantage of assured shorthold tenancies by size of landlords total lettings portfolio

Advantages of assured shorthold tenancies	Total number of lettings				
	1	2-7	8-40	41+	All
Easier/guaranteed repossession at end of lease	79%	88%	80%	75%	80%
Fixed term tenancies - can review situation at end of lease	11%	4%	8%	18%	11%
Can charge market rents/can set own rent level	2%	3%	9%	17%	9%
Greater mutual awareness of rights	8%	12%	8%	6%	8%
Generally feel more in control/greater flexibility/easier to manage property	3%	4%	8%	10%	7%
No advantages	2%	1%	2%	4%	3%
Other	-	-	1%	1%	1%
Vague/irrelevant/unspecific	3%	1%	-	2%	2%
Don't know	2%	-	2%	1%	1%
Not answered	2%	1%	3%	1%	2%
Base	62	69	86	108	325

Base: all lettings whose landlords let on assured shorthold tenancies

Table 9.17 : Advantage of assured shorthold tenancies by type of landlord

Advantages	Landlord type				
	Sideline sample letting		Business	Institution	All
	Non-investment	Investment			
Easier/guaranteed repossession at end of lease	75%	83%	82%	77%	80%
Fixed term tenancies - can review situation at end of lease	9%	12%	9%	23%	11%
Can charge market rents/can set own rent level/can charge higher rent	7%	7%	16%	6%	9%
Greater mutual awareness of rights	8%	13%	4%	3%	8%
Generally feel more in control/greater flexibility/easier to manage property	9%	3%	9%	10%	7%
No advantages	1%	2%	5%	6%	3%
Other	2%	-	-	-	1%
Vague/irrelevant/unspecific	2%	1%	3%	-	1%
Don't know	2%	2%	-	-	1%

Not answered	2%	2%	1%	-	2%
Base	98	119	77	31	235

Base: all lettings whose landlords let on assured shorthold tenancies

Table 9.18 : Advantage of assured shortholding tenancies by 'old' and 'new' landlords

Advantages	Old landlord	New landlord
Easier/guaranteed repossession at end of lease	80%	80%
Fixed term tenancies - can review situation at end of lease	10%	8%
Can charge market rents/can set own rent level	10%	4%
Greater mutual awareness of rights	9%	8%
Generally feel more in control/greater flexibility to manage property	7%	5%
No advantages	3%	3%
Other	1%	-
Vague/irrelevant/unspecific	1%	1%
Don't know	1%	1%
Not answered	2%	1%
Base	219	73

Base: all lettings whose landlords let on assured shorthold tenancies

9.37 Flexibility was also explicitly mentioned as an advantage by the landlords of 7% of lettings and by the agents of 5%. They felt more in control, had greater flexibility and found it easier to manage property. A related advantage mentioned by the landlords of 8% of lettings and by the agents of 17% of lettings was that landlords and tenants had a greater mutual awareness of their rights.

9.38 Whilst the ability to charge market rents or to set their own rent levels was mentioned by comparatively few landlords and agents (at least in comparison with the overwhelming majority who mentioned getting easier repossession), it was an advantage noted more by agents than by landlords (Table 9.15) and more by larger portfolios than by smaller landlords (Table 9.16).

Assured shorthold tenancies: disadvantages

9.39 Over half the landlords with experience of letting on assured shorthold tenancies said that this form of letting had no disadvantages, and so too did the agents of 43% of the lettings (Table 9.19). Approximately the same proportions of landlords of all types and portfolio sizes said there were no disadvantages (Tables 9.20 and 9.21). Seventy % of lettings with new landlords had owners who said there were no disadvantages, compared with just over half those with old (long-standing) landlords (Table 9.22).

Table 9.19 : Disadvantages of assured shorthold tenancies

Disadvantages	Landlords	Agents
No disadvantages	58%	43%
Still difficult to get possession/court procedures too long/costly	13%	15%
High tenant turnover/tenancies too short	6%	5%
Cannot arrange let of < 6 months	5%	11%
Problems with form filling/drawing up agreement/too complacent	4%	2%
Tenants do not have long term security	4%	5%
Have to serve at least 2 months notice to end tenancy	3%	5%
Tenants can go to rent assessment panel	<1%	5%
Other	6%	12%
Vague/irrelevant/unspecific	2%	1%
Don't know	2%	1%
Not answered	2%	2%
Base	325	255

Base: all lettings whose landlords or agents let on assured shorthold tenancies

9.40 Those who said there were no disadvantages were less likely to have experienced problems with letting accommodation since 1988. For example only 24% of lettings whose landlords said there were no disadvantages had a problem regaining possession since 1988, compared with 51% of those who identified one or more disadvantages.

Table 9.20 : Disadvantages of assured shorthold tenancies by size of landlords total lettings portfolio

Disadvantages	Total number of lettings				
	1	2-7	8-40	41+	All
No disadvantages	64%	64%	57%	52%	58%
Still difficult to get possession/court procedures too long/costly	18%	10%	13%	11%	13%
High tenant turnover/tenancies too short	6%	3%	6%	7%	6%
Cannot arrange let of < 6 months	6%	6%	3%	6%	5%
Problems with form filling/drawing up arrangement/too complicated	-	4%	5%	6%	4%
Tenants do not have long term security	-	1%	1%	9%	4%
Have to serve at least 2 months notice to end tenancy	2%	1%	5%	3%	3%

	Non-invest-ment				
Tenants can go to rent assessment panel	-	-	-	2%	<1%
Other	-	3%	7%	12%	6%
Vague/irrelevant/unspecific	2%	3%	3%	2%	2%
Don't know	5%	4%	2%	-	2%
Not answered	2%	1%	3%	2%	2%
Base	62	69	86	108	325

Base: all lettings whose landlords or agents let on assured shorthold lettings

Table 9.21 : Disadvantages of assured shorthold tenancies by type of landlords

Disadvantages of assured shorthold tenancies	Landlord type				
	Sideline sample letting		Business	Institu-tion	All
	Non-invest-ment	Invest-ment			
No disadvantages	57%	60%	60%	52%	58%
Still difficult to get possession/court procedures too long/costly	13%	10%	17%	10%	13%
High tenant turnover/tenancies too short	6%	7%	5%	3%	6%
Cannot arrange let of < 6 months	6%	4%	1%	16%	5%
Problems with form filling/drawing up agreement/too complicated	6%	3%	4%	-	4%
Tenants do not have long term security	2%	3%	3%	13%	4%
Have to serve at least 2 months notice to end tenancy	1%	4%	1%	6%	3%
Tenants can go to rent assessment panel	1%	-	-	-	<1%
Other	7%	5%	6%	10%	6%
Vague/irrelevant/unspecific	1%	3%	4%	-	2%
Don't know	3%	2%	3%	-	2%
Not answered	2%	2%	3%	-	2%
Sample numbers	98	119	77	31	325

Base: all lettings whose landlords let on assured shorthold tenancies

Table 9.22 : Disadvantage of assured shorthold tenancies by 'old' and 'new' landlords		
Disadvantages	'Old' landlords	'New' landlords
No disadvantages	56%	70%
Still difficult to get possession/court procedures too long/costly	14%	11%
High tenant turnover/tenancies too short	6%	4%
Cannot arrange let of < 6 months	6%	4%
Problems with form filling/drawing up agreement/too complicated	5%	4%
Tenants do not have long term security	3%	1%
Have to serve at least 2 months notice to end tenancy	3%	1%
Tenants can go to rent assessment panel	1%	-
Other	7%	1%
Vague/irrelevant/unspecific	2%	3%
Don't know	2%	1%
Not answered	2%	1%
Base	219	73

Base: all lettings whose landlords let on assured shorthold tenancies

9.41 As Table 9.19 shows, those landlords and agents who identified disadvantages cited a wide range of them, but they were almost all related to issues surrounding security of tenure and getting possession rather than rents. The landlords of 13% lettings (and the agents of about 15% lettings) said that it was still difficult for them to get possession and that court procedures were too long and costly, a view held in about the same proportion by all types and portfolio sizes of landlords.

9.42 The agents of 11% of lettings said they could not arrange lets of less than six months (which some agents had identified as one of the advantages of assured tenancies - see above). However, in contrast about one in 20 lettings had landlords and agents who remarked that the tenancies were too short (sic) and/or led to high tenant turnover (confirming that minimising turnover may be an important factor for some landlords and agents). Indeed, 4% of lettings also had landlords, and 5% had agents, who noted that one disadvantage of assured shorthold tenancies was that tenants did not have security, a point made more by larger portfolio landlords than smaller ones (of all types), providing some indication of a 'portfolio effect'.

9.43 Other disadvantages were related to the 'paperwork' associated with this type of agreement. Small proportions noted the need to serve two months notice in order to terminate assured shorthold tenancies and to the problems associated with form filling and drawing up complicated agreements. These clearly have presented problems to those who have experienced them, but this evidence suggest, nonetheless, that the 'bureaucracy' of assured shortholds does not present itself as a disadvantage to all but the landlords and agents of a small minority of lettings (and does not appear to be a disadvantage mentioned more by smaller than by larger landlords).

9.44 Similarly, issues related to rents hardly featured at all amongst landlords and the agents of only 5% of lettings noted that tenants could refer rents to a rent assessment panel as one of the disadvantages of assured shortholds.

Changes since 1988

9.45 Given that there had been many changes to the environment for letting since 1988 (including the legal framework discussed above, but also many other changes, for example the slump in the owner occupied market), landlords and agents were also asked whether they felt the situation for landlords had changed in any way to their advantage over the last six years (since 1988). They were, in addition, asked if the situation had changed in any way to their disadvantage.

Table 9.23 : Had the situation changed since 1988 to landlords' advantage?					
		Yes	No	Don't know	Base
Landlords	%	47	29	23	(543)
Agents	%	81	14	4	(270)
Base: all lettings					

9.46 Nearly half of all lettings had landlords who said that the situation had changed to their advantage. Twenty-nine % had owners who said that it had not, and just under a quarter did not know (Table 9.23). It will be noted that the agents of 81% of lettings thought there had been change to landlords' advantage. Only 14% said not. Only four % did not know, a much smaller proportion than landlords, reflecting, perhaps, their greater level of knowledge about changes, compared with landlords.

9.47 There were also significant differences between different types and portfolio sizes of landlords (Table 9.24). First, half the lettings whose landlords had been letting before deregulation ('old' landlords) had owners who said the situation had changed to their advantage, compared with only a third of lettings whose landlords had started letting on or after deregulation ('new' landlords). Perhaps, not surprisingly, over a third of lettings with new landlords had owners who did not know, possibly because they had not been letting long enough to consider the impact of changes upon them.

Table 9.24 : Had the situation changed since 1988 to landlords' advantage by characteristic of landlords

			Yes	No	Don't know	Base
(a)	'Old' landlords	%	51	30	20	(377)
	'New' landlords	%	34	31	35	(119)
(b)	*Size of total lettings portfolio*					
	1	%	31	27	41	(138)
	2-7	%	41	40	19	(122)
	8-40	%	58	26	16	(123)
	41+	%	60	24	16	(150)
(c)	*Type of landlord*					
	Sideline - noninvestment	%	39	33	27	(197)
	Sideline - investment	%	47	32	22	(184)
	Business	%	70	19	11	(103)
	Institutional	%	39	24	37	(59)
(d)	*Investment orientation*					
	Growth seeker	%	56	22	22	(100)
	Income seeker	%	56	31	13	(183)
	Slump victim	%	54	29	17	(24)
	Employer	%	40	25	34	(67)
	Other	%	3	34	32	(167)

Base: all lettings where landlord interviewed

9.48 It will also be noted that a greater proportion of lettings owned by landlords with larger rather than smaller portfolios had owners who said there had been change to their advantage: for example, 60% of lettings with landlords who owned 41 or more lettings, compared with only 41% of lettings whose landlords owned between two and seven lettings throughout England.

9.49 Moreover a greater proportion of lettings owned by business (70%) than by other types of landlords, had landlords who said changes had been to landlords' advantage. Over half of all lettings whose landlords sought capital growth and income had owners who said changes had been to their advantage.

Table 9.25 : Ways in which the situation had changed to the advantage of landlords' since 1988	Landlord	Agent
Introduction of assured shorthold	40%	52%
Easier repossession/easier to evict undesirable tenants	34%	52%
Can charge market/higher/more realistic rents	26%	37%
Private renting move acceptable/less stigma	6%	11%
More control/protection/flexibility	5%	2%
Shorter tenancies, including more flexibility/control as a result	3%	8%
Reduced interest rates	2%	1%
Fall in property values	2%	1%
Introduction of 'poll'/council tax	1%	1%
Increased repairs/improvement grants	1%	1%
Tenants have more security	<1%	<1%
Capital gains tax charges	<1%	<1%
Other	4%	10%
Vague	1%	-
Don't know	-	-
Not answered	1%	-

Base: all lettings whose landlords said changes were advantageous

9.50 Table 9.25 lists the ways landlords and agents said the situation had changed to their advantage. Most of the changes listed were mentioned by the landlords and agents of only a very small proportion of addresses, but five ways were mentioned by more: three were related to security of tenure for tenants; one to rents; and one to the image of private renting. All portfolio sizes and types of landlords mentioned these in approximately the same proportions.

9.51 First, 40% and 52% of lettings had, respectively, landlords and agents who explicitly mentioned the introduction of assured shortholds. Second, over a third, 34%, had landlords and over a half, 52%, had agents who mentioned that there was easier repossession in general or specifically that it was easier to evict undesirable tenants. Third, 3% and 8% had landlords and agents, respectively, who identified that they could let on shorter tenancies, including the way that gave them more flexibility and control as a result.

9.52 Fourth, just over a quarter of lettings (26%) had landlords who noted that changes meant they were able to charge market rents (or higher or more realistic rents). Over a third of lettings (37%) also had agents who noted this.

133

9.53 Fifth, 6% of lettings had landlords and 11% had agents who said that private renting had become more acceptable and had less stigma than in 1988.

Table 9.26 : Had the situation changed since 1988 to landlords disadvantage?		Yes	No	Don't know	Base
Landlords	%	24	50	26	(543)
Agents	%	30	64	6	(270)
Base: all lettings					

9.54 As Table 9.26 shows, only 24% of lettings had landlords who said that the situation had changed to their disadvantage since 1988 (only half the proportion whose landlords said things had changed to their advantage). Half said that the situation had not changed to their disadvantage. The agents of only 30% of lettings said the situation had changed to the disadvantage of landlords. Nearly two thirds had agents who said it had not changed to their disadvantage.

9.56 Thus the proportion of lettings with landlords and agents who said the situation had not changed to their disadvantage was twice that of those with landlords and agents who said that it had. Only 25% of lettings whose landlords had said there had been changes to their advantage since 1988 also said that there had been changes to their disadvantage. Moreover half those who said that there had been no changes to their advantage also said that there had been no changes to their disadvantage.

Table 9.27 : Had the situation changed since 1988 to landlords' disadvantage by characteristic of landlords		Yes	No	Don't know	Base
(a) 'Old' landlords	%	25	54	21	(377)
'New' landlords	%	21	36	43	(119)
(b) Size of total lettings portfolio					
1	%	11	41	49	(138)
2-7	%	21	56	23	(122)
8-40	%	34	51	15	(123)
41+	%	30	54	16	(150)
(c) Type of landlord					
Sideline - noninvestment	%	19	46	34	(197)
Sideline - investment	%	24	55	21	(184)

Business	%	36	54	10	(103)
Institution	%	15	44	41	(59)
(d) *Investment orientation*					
Growth seeker	%	24	58	18	(100)
Income seeker	%	31	55	14	(183)
Slump victim	%	17	42	42	(24)
Employer	%	13	51	36	(67)
Other	%	21	42	37	(167)

Base: all lettings where landlord interviewed

9.57 Although roughly similar proportion of 'old' and 'new' landlords thought things had changed to their disadvantage, over 43% of the lettings owned by 'new' landlords had owners who did not know whether things had changed in this way or not (Table 9.27). As Table 9.27 also shows, larger portfolio, business landlords and those seeking capital growth or an income, were all more likely than other landlords to say things had changed to their disadvantage, although in much smaller proportions than had said that changes had been advantageous.

9.58 A wide range of 'disadvantageous' changes were mentioned, and these are listed in Table 9.28. In only a few cases were some changes mentioned more by some types of landlords than others (and these are noted below).

Table 9.28 : Ways in which situations had changed to the disadvantage of landlords since 1988

	Landlord	Agent
Harder to let because of increased competition/higher standards	17%	31%
Not enough protection for landlords/ law too much in tenants' favour	17%	9%
Rents increased less than inflation	14%	15%
Recession/adverse economic conditions	14%	16%
Difficulty in repossessing property/court procedures too long/costly	11%	11%
More stringent environment health regulations	10%	12%
Reduced availability of repairs/improvement grants	7%	6%
Problems with Housing Benefit	5%	-
Introduction of shorter tenancies	2%	5%
Abolition of rent control/fair rents/rents too high	2%	4%
Other	25%	29%

Vague	-	4%
Don't know	-	-
Not answered	-	-

Base: all lettings whose landlords said changes were disadvantageous

9.59 The change mentioned in the greatest proportion by both landlords and agents was that it was harder to let than in the past, because of greater competition and because higher standards were being sought by tenants. This was noted by the landlords of 17% of lettings and by as many as the agents of 31% of lettings.

9.60 Some of the changes noted were related to the legal framework for letting. Just over 11% of lettings had landlords and agents who mentioned their difficulty in repossessing property and the fact that court procedures had been long and costly. Fourteen % of lettings had landlords (and 15% had agents) who referred in a general way to the fact that there was not enough protection for landlords and that the law was too much in tenants' favour.

9.61 Small proportions (the landlords of two % of lettings in each case) mentioned that the introduction of 'shorter' tenancies and the abolition of rent control had been to their disadvantage. These points were only made by sideline landlords who did not regard the sample letting as an investment and by institutional landlords, reflecting the concern that these landlords may have had about the impact of changes upon their tenants.

9.62 Five % of lettings had landlords who were concerned about problems they had with Housing Benefit - all of these were 'old' more long-standing landlords.

9.63 Another set of changes were related to building fabric. The reduced availability of improvement and repairs grants were noted by the owners of 7% of lettings and 10% of lettings had landlords who mentioned more stringent environmental health regulations.

9.64 Finally, approximately the same proportion, 14%, of lettings had landlords (and agents) who mentioned two specific financial and economic changes - that rents had increased less than inflation and that they had been affected by the adverse economic conditions in the recession. These changes were mentioned more by new than by old landlords.

10 Letting strategies

Summary

10.1 The main findings of this chapter are:

- the households that landlords and agents most preferred covered a wide range of household types;

- they least preferred to let to young single people and households with children;

- they most preferred to let to those in work and least preferred to let to students, the unemployed and others outside the labour market.

Introduction

10.2   When deciding to let accommodation, landlords and their agents have a wide range of decisions to make - about rents and the types of letting agreement to use, for example. They may also wish to consider whether there are certain kinds of potential tenants they would particularly wish to accommodate - or to avoid.

10.3   They may, for example, be keen to let only to 'short stay' tenants if they want to keep open their short term options about the use of their property. On the other hand they may wish to avoid such tenants because their rapid turnover increases, potentially at least, void periods and costs of repairs and decorations between tenancies. They may also want to select tenants who they think will care for the property, thus minimising landlords' costs.

10.4   Moreover, the small scale nature of the private rented sector and the fact that many landlords look after their property themselves means that landlords may well want to consider how they are likely to 'get on' with potential tenants, because their personal relationships may affect the ease with which property can be 'managed'. Where the accommodation is shared by several households, landlords may also need to take account of the potential for friction or harmony between existing and new, potential, tenants. It may be in their best interests to do this both to minimise rent loss, if friction results in tenants leaving, and to reduce landlords' time sorting out disputes between tenants.

10.5   As Chapter 3 has shown, landlords have a great diversity of motives in letting accommodation, so that their considerations about to whom to let are likely to incorporate far more than void periods, cash flow matters and personal time commitment.

10.6   Previous chapters have examined rents and letting arrangements at the sample lettings. The last chapter looked at landlords' and agents' views on types of letting agreement. This chapter examines landlords' and agents' preferences for different types of household and tenant. In doing so, it does not necessarily provide information about who is housed in the sector. Whether or not landlords' preferences can be achieved depends on the demand for what they have on offer. It may well be that they are unable to attract those they would ideally wish to accommodate and thus let to others.

10.7 Like the last chapter, the information in this chapter is based upon landlords' and agents' views in general, not about their preferences when letting the specific accommodation sampled in the course of this survey.

Types of household

10.8 Landlords and agents were asked whom they would most and least prefer to let to when letting accommodation. They were asked both about household types and about tenants' economic status. In each case they were asked to select the one type of household or tenant they most or least preferred from a list given to them. This section describes what they said about household types.

Table 10.1 : The type of tenant *household* landlords and agents *most* preferred	Landlords	Agents
	%	%
A couple with no children	22	32
Middle aged single people	16	11
A couple with children	13	15
Elderly people	8	8
Young single people	7	4
Households without children generally	5	4
Lone parents	1	2
No preference	21	18
Other	2	3
Can't say	4	3
Not applicable	1	-
Base	543	270
Base: all lettings		

10.9 As Table 10.1 shows, landlords and agents most preferred a wide range of household types, although about 20% of lettings had landlords and agents who had no preference. Landlords who had no preference were more likely to be larger landlords, suggesting that some of the risks associated with having particular types of households can be diversified within a large portfolio (Table 10.2). This was particularly the case for sideline landlords. Those without preferences were also more likely to be institutional landlords (Table 10.3) and this was true irrespective of their portfolio size, 47% of lettings owned by institutions having landlords with no preference.

Table 10.2 : The type of tenant *household*, landlords *most* preferred by size of landlords' total lettings portfolio

Household type	Total lettings				
	1	2-7	8-40	41+	All
	%	%	%	%	%
A couple with no children	26	22	21	19	22
Middle aged single people	17	22	19	7	16
A couple with children	14	13	11	14	13
Elderly people	6	10	8	8	8
Young single people	6	8	10	3	7
Households without children generally	6	7	4	5	5
Lone parents	1	-	2	1	1
No preference	17	15	19	31	21
Other	2	1	-	3	2
Can't say	4	1	6	6	4
Not applicable	-	1	1	1	1
Base	138	132	123	150	543

Base: all lettings where landlord interviewed

10.10 Over a fifth of lettings had landlords who most preferred couples without children and a third of lettings had agents who had this preference (Table 10.1). One in 20 lettings had landlords and agents who most preferred households without children, regardless of whether the other members were couples. With the exception of institutional landlords, only 9% of whom preferred childless households, there were no major differences in the proportions of landlords preferring such households, whatever the size of the total lettings portfolio or type, although there was a tendency for landlords with smaller portfolios to have a greater preference for childless couples than others (Tables 10.2 and 10.3).

Household type	Type of landlord				
	Sideline sample letting		Business	Institutional	All
	Non-investment	Investment			
	%	%	%	%	%
A couple with no children	25	24	22	7	22
Middle aged single people	15	20	15	5	16
A couple with children	12	14	15	10	13
Elderly people	8	7	13	3	8
Young single people	5	9	8	3	7
Households without children generally	7	5	6	2	5
Lone parents	1	2	1	-	1
No preference	22	15	14	47	21
Other	2	1	-	7	2
Can't say	4	2	5	14	4
Not applicable	<1	<1	1	2	1
Base	197	184	103	59	543

Table 10.3 : The type of tenant *household* landlords *most* preferred by type of landlord

Base: all lettings where landlord interviewed

10.11 In contrast, 13% of lettings had landlords who preferred couples with children, as did the agents of 15% of lettings. This was a preference of landlords of all types and sizes in approximately similar proportions. Only 1% of lettings had landlords who preferred lone parents - and only 2% had agents who held this view.

10.12 Although nearly a quarter of lettings (23%) had landlords who most preferred single people (as did the agents of 11% of lettings), most of this was a preference for middle aged single people (16% in the case of landlords), rather than young single people (7%). Thus, only a small minority of lettings had landlords and agents who most preferred young singles, despite the fact that they are one of the largest groups of tenants within the sector. This was the case for all types and sizes of landlords.

10.13 Just under one in 10 of lettings had landlords and agents (8%) who most preferred to let to elderly people.

Table 10.4 : The type of tenant *household* landlords and agents *least* preferred

Household	Landlords	Agents
	%	%
Young single people	38	38
A couple with children	14	5
Lone parents	14	25
Elderly people	5	7
Middle aged single people	1	2
Households without children generally	<1	<1
A couple with no children	-	-
No preference	21	16
Other	2	3
Can't say	5	3
Not applicable	1	<1
Base	543	270
Base: all lettings		

10.14 The types of households least preferred are shown in Table 10.4, where it will be seen that a fifth of lettings (21%) had landlords with no preference against any of the types listed (as did the agents of 16% of lettings). Larger portfolio and institutional landlords were most likely to have no household type they least preferred (Tables 10.5 and 10.6).

Table 10.5 : The types of tenant *household* landlords *least* preferred by size of landlords' total lettings portfolio

Household type	Total lettings				
	1	2-7	8-40	41+	All
	%	%	%	%	%
Young single people	43	39	37	31	38
A couple with children	13	23	16	7	14
Lone parents	12	12	16	15	14
Elderly people	5	4	5	6	5
Middle aged single people	1	1	-	1	1
Households without children generally	-	-	-	1	<1

A couple with no children	-	-	-	-	-
No preference	18	15	21	27	21
Other	3	3	-	1	2
Can't say	4	1	4	9	5
Not applicable	1	1	-	3	1
Base	138	132	123	150	543

Base: all lettings where landlord interviewed

Table 10.6 : The types of tenant household landlords least preferred by type of landlord

Household type	Type of landlord				
	Sideline sample letting		Business	Institutional	All
	Non-investment	Investment			
	%	%	%	%	%
Young single people	36	43	43	19	38
A couple with children	17	16	15	2	14
Lone parents	12	14	19	10	14
Elderly people	6	4	8	2	5
Middle aged single people	-	2	-	-	1
Households without children generally	-	<1	1	-	<1
A couple with no children	-	-	-	-	-
No preference	22	16	12	46	21
Other	1	3	1	-	2
Can't say	5	2	2	17	5
Not applicable	1	<1	-	5	1
Base	197	184	103	59	543

Base: all lettings where landlord interviewed

10.15 However, three household types were least preferred by the landlords and agents of most of the rest of the lettings. These were young single people, couples with children and lone parents.

10.16 The landlords and the agents of nearly four in 10 lettings least preferred young single people (despite their significant presence within the sector), a preference held more by smaller than by larger portfolio landlords (Tables 10.4 and 10.5). Fourteen % of lettings had landlords who least preferred lone parents, as did the agents of a quarter of lettings. Couples with children were least preferred by the owners of 14% of lettings and the agents of 5%. However, smaller proportions of larger portfolio and of sideline and institutional than of other sizes and types of landlord least preferred couples with children (Tables 10.4 to 10.6). About 1 in 20 lettings had landlords who least preferred the elderly.

Types of tenant: economic status

10.17 Whereas as many as one in five lettings had landlords who did not have a preference for letting to particular household types (Table 10.1), only one in 10 had no preference as far as tenants' economic status is concerned (Table 10.7).

Table 10.7 : The type of tenant landlords and agents *most* preferred		
Economic status of tenant	Landlords	Agents
	%	%
People in work	56	71
Own employees	14	10
Retired people	8	5
Students	4	2
Overseas visitors	2	3
Unemployed people	1	1
Long term sick/disabled	1	-
People on government training schemes	<1	-
No preference	10	6
Other	1	2
Can't say	2	1
Not applicable	1	-
Base	543	270
Base: all lettings		

10.18 Landlords and agents mainly preferred those with jobs. As Table 10.7 shows, the landlords of over half lettings (56%) and the agents of over 70% of lettings most preferred to let to people in work. Very few indeed, only 1%, of lettings had landlords or agents who preferred unemployed people.

10.19 In addition, as would be expected, a significant proportion most preferred to let to their own employees. Fourteen % of lettings had landlords with this preference (Table 10.7). The agents of 10% of lettings most preferred to let to their clients' employees.

10.20 Very few lettings had landlords or agents who most preferred those outside the labour market. Only a small proportion, 4%, of lettings had landlords or agents who most preferred to let to students, although 18% of lettings had landlords preferring to let to those who were retired. Small proportions preferred the long term sick and overseas visitors (Table 10.7).

10.21 The size of landlords' property holding was not strongly related to preferences, with the exception of the housing of employees, who were most preferred more by larger than smaller landlords (Table 10.8). This reflects the numbers of large institutional landlords in the sector and Table 10.9 shows that institutional (as well as sideline landlords who did not own the sample letting for investment reasons) were more likely to prefer their own employees than were other types of landlord.

Table 10.8 : The type of tenant that landlord *most* preferred by size of landlords' total lettings portfolio

Economic status of tenant	Total lettings				
	1	2-7	8-40	41+	All
	%	%	%	%	%
People in work	59	65	59	43	56
Own employees	7	7	15	25	14
Retired people	7	10	4	9	8
Students	2	7	2	3	4
Overseas visitors	3	1	1	1	2
Unemployed people	1	2	2	-	1
Long term sick/disabled	1	1	2	-	1
People on government training scheme	1	-	-	-	<1
No preference	12	6	10	11	10
Other	3	1	-	2	1
Can't say	3	-	2	3	2
Not applicable	-	-	2	2	1
Base	138	132	123	150	543

Base: all lettings whose landlord interviewed

10.22 However, there were not many other strong differences in the preferences of different types of landlords. It will be noted that nearly 7% of sideline landlords with investment motives and business landlords preferred those in work. It will also be noted that very few business landlords preferred students: if anything they were more likely (though not to a great extent) to be preferred by sideline landlords with investment motives and by institutions (presumably their universities and colleges) (Table 10.9). On the other hand business landlords were more likely than others to most prefer the retired.

Economic status of tenant	Type of landlord				
	Sideline sample letting		Business	Institution	All
	Non-investment	Investment			
	%	%	%	%	%
People in work	50	68	68	19	56
Own employees	22	5	4	30	14
Retired people	5	9	14	2	8
Students	2	5	2	8	4
Overseas visitors	2	-	2	3	2
Unemployed people	1	2	1	-	1
Long term sick/disabled	1	<1	2	-	1
People on government training scheme	1	-	-	-	<1
No preference	10	8	5	24	10
Other	2	<1	-	3	1
Can't say	2	<1	2	7	2
Not applicable	-	1	1	3	1
Base	197	184	103	59	543

Table 10.9 : The type of tenant landlords *most* preferred by type of landlord

Base: all lettings where landlords interviewed

10.23 But these differences are relatively minor. The main finding is that preferences for people in the labour market (but not the unemployed), including landlords' own staff, dominated landlords' and agents' views.

10.24 Not surprisingly, therefore, landlords and agents least preferred to let to the unemployed and students (and also to the long term sick and disabled) (Table 10.10). Over a quarter of lettings had landlords who least preferred unemployed people and over a third of lettings had agents with this preference. Similarly the landlords of a quarter of lettings preferred not to let to students, as did the agents of 29% of lettings (Table 10.10).

Table 10.10 : The type of tenant landlords and agents *least* preferred		
Economic status of tenant	Landlords	Agents
	%	%
Unemployed people	27	37
Students	24	29
Long term sick/disabled	12	7
Overseas visitors	10	11
Own employees	2	3
People in work	1	-
People on government training scheme	1	2
Retired people	1	<1
No preference	13	8
Other	2	<1
Can't say	6	2
Not applicable	1	1
Base	543	270

10.25 There were very minor and insignificant variations in the preferences of landlords of different sizes and types, except that over a third of lettings owned by institutions had landlords who had no preference against tenants of any economic status.

Tenants that landlords and agents did not want

10.26 As well as asking landlords and agents about the sorts of households and tenants they most and least preferred, they were also asked if there were any tenants they would definitely not want. Their answers are listed in Table 10.11. As many as 3 in 10 of lettings had agents and landlords who said that there was no one kind of tenant they would not let to, a proportion that was similar for all sizes and types of landlords. However, only 20% of lettings whose landlords had shared accommodation had owners who said that there was no one they would not let to, compared with 32% of lettings whose landlords had no shared accommodation in England. This lends some support to the argument that some landlords with shared lettings take account of the personal characteristics of their tenants in order to foster harmonious relationships between them.

Table 10.11 : Kinds of tenants that landlords and agents definitely did *not* want

Kind of tenant	Landlords	Agents
	%	%
None	30	28
Students/young sharers	12	15
Drug addicts/alcoholics	10	4
Unemployed	8	18
Troublesome/untidy tenants	8	7
Hippies/new age travellers/tramps	6	7
Overseas visitors/foreigners/immigrants	6	7
People with prison/policy record	5	6
Elderly people/long term sick or disabled	5	3
Any nonemployee	4	1
Tenants who don't pay rent	4	6
Tenants on Housing Benefit or Income Support	3	7
People with unsatisfactory references	3	11
Tenants with children/large families	3	3
Tenants with pets	3	4
Single parents	2	3
Mentally ill	2	1
People with bad debts	1	4
Unmarried couples	<1	-
Other	9	10
Vague	1	1
Don't know	1	<1
Not answered	1	1
Base	543	270

Base: all lettings

10.27 Apart from mentioning students and the unemployed (whom the landlords of 12% and eight % respectively of lettings would not take on), the other kinds of tenants listed were those who experienced a wide range of social, economic or behavioural difficulties. It is noticeable however, that none of the kinds listed in Table 10.11 was mentioned by anything other than a small minority of landlords and agents. Agents, however, were more likely than landlords to not want to let to the unemployed, those receiving Housing Benefit or Income Support, with bad debts or unsatisfactory references.

Ease of letting to preferred tenants

10.28 The landlords of a third (32%) and the agents of 20% of lettings said it was a very easy to let to the households and types of tenants they preferred. The landlords and agents of 40% and 20% respectively said it was fairly easy. Only small proportions said it was fairly or very difficult (Table 10.12). The ease with which accommodation could be let was not related to the type of household and tenant preferred by landlords and agents. In other words they said it was as easy (or difficult) to let, whichever they most preferred. Nor did the region where their sample letting was located make any difference to the ease of letting. It was as easy (or difficult) to let to those they preferred wherever they provided accommodation.

Table 10.12 : The ease with which landlords and agents were able to let to the types of tenants they wanted

Ease	Landlord	Agent
	%	%
Very easy	32	20
Fairly easy	40	60
Fairly difficult	11	15
Very difficult	4	1
Not applicable/can't say	13	4
Base	543	270
Base: all lettings		

11   Landlords' difficulties

Summary

11.1   The main findings of this chapter are:

- Problems with respect to arrears, difficult tenants and regaining possession are the most common problems for landlords and agents;

- A large proportion of landlords and agents seek advice about their problems, predominantly from solicitors and most find the advice they get is helpful;

- Nearly all agents and nearly half landlords have asked tenants.to leave on at least one occasion since 1988;

- The main reason for asking tenants to leave was rent arrears;

- three in 10 of landlords and eight in 10 of agents have taken court action at least once since 1988.

Introduction

11.2   Very little is known about the extent to which landlords experience problems when letting accommodation (for example, deciding what agreements to use, dealing with arrears, or sorting out tax bills on rental income) nor about the sources of advice they use. An attempt to fill this important gap in our knowledge was therefore made in the interviews with landlords and agents in the recent lettings survey, when they were asked about the problems they experienced and the advice they used to tackle these.

11.3   This chapter looks at:

- the extent to which landlords and agents had experienced problems during the six year period since deregulation;

- whether landlords and agents sought advice about these problems, and from whom, and whether they found the advice helpful;

- whether landlords and agents had asked tenants to leave since deregulation and whether court action had been taken against tenants;

Problems experienced by landlords and agents

11.4   Landlords were explicitly asked if they had a problem about each of the matters listed in Table 11.1. The list contains many of the problems which landlords and landlords' organisations have identified as typical of the problems which landlords regularly have to deal with, not withstanding the changes made in 1989 to the framework within which landlords let accommodation.

11.5   The extent of these problems varies significantly (Table 11.1). Over 40% of addresses where landlords were interviewed had owners who had problems about dealing with arrears and with difficult tenants and 30% had owners who had problems regaining possession. Problems involved in bringing agreements to an end affected 21%, whilst problems with the types of agreement to use and getting repairs or improvement grants affected 16%. Problems with renewing tenancy agreements and the taxation of their rental income affected relatively few (5 and 9% respectively). Thus three types of problems - arrears, difficult tenants and regaining repossession - were much more widespread than others.

Table 11.1 : Proportion of addresses whose landlords and agents had problems since 1988	Landlords	Agents
Dealing with difficult tenants	44%	81%
Dealing with rent arrears	43%	82%
Regaining possession	30%	56%
Bringing an agreement to an end	21%	38%
Types of agreement used	16%	10%
Getting a grant for repairs or improvement	16%	24%
Taxation of rental income	9%	17%
Renewing a tenancy agreement	5%	9%
Base	331	181

Base: interviews with all landlords and all agents

11.6   Not surprisingly, given the likelihood that they were dealing with a much larger number of properties than landlords, agents had experienced problems to a much greater extent since 1988. For example over 80% of the addresses managed by agents had managers who had problems dealing with arrears or with difficult tenants and over half had problems regaining possession. Only the case of deciding what types of agreements to use had proportionately fewer agents than landlords had problems (Table 11.1).

11.7   There were also significant differences in the extent to which different types of landlords had experienced problems. In general, business, institutional landlords and sideline landlords whose sample addresses were investments were more likely than other sideline landlords to have experienced problems. For example, two thirds of the addresses with business landlords had owners who had problems since 1988 dealing with arrears, compared with less than 30% of those owned by sideline landlords (Table 11.2).

Table 11.2 : Proportion of addresses whose landlords had problems since 1988 by type of landlord				
	Sideline sample letting		Business	Institutional
	Non-investment	Investment		
Dealing with difficult tenants	32%	41%	63%	54%
Dealing with rent arrears	29%	44%	67%	43%
Regaining possession	19%	31%	41%	43%
Bringing an agreement to an end	17%	20%	27%	22%
Types of agreement used	17%	16%	16%	13%
Getting a grant for repairs or improvement	12%	17%	21%	16%
Taxation of rental income	7%	10%	11%	5%
Renewing a tenancy agreement	3%	5%	2%	13%
Base	113	118	63	37

Base: interviews with all landlords and all agents

11.8   Not unexpectedly, landlords with larger portfolios were more likely to have had to deal with problems than those with smaller ones, especially in the case of those problems which were the most widespread (arrears, difficult tenants, and regaining repossession). For example, only 11% of landlords with just one property had had a difficulty with arrears at that property, whereas over 70% of the addresses whose landlords had more than 40 properties had owners who had experienced problems with arrears (Table 11.3). By contrast, where problems were not widespread (deciding on the type of agreement to use, renewing agreements and dealing with taxation), addresses belonging to landlords with larger portfolios did not seem more likely to have owners with these problems than those with landlords who had fewer lettings. However, size seemed to be a factor which was related to the extent of problems faced by sideline, rather than by business landlords, because the proportion of the latter experiencing problems was not as strongly related to size as it was with the former. For example over half business landlords experienced problems with arrears, whatever their size, whereas only a quarter of sideline landlords with seven or fewer addresses had problems with arrears, compared with over six in 10 of those with eight or more lettings.

Table 11.3 : Proportion of addresses whose landlords had problems since 1988 by size of landlords' total lettings portfolio

	Size of lettings portfolio			
	1	2-7	8-40	41+
Dealing with difficult tenants	12%	44%	50%	73%
Dealing with rent arrears	11%	46%	50%	70%
Regaining possession	8%	19%	45%	54%
Bringing an agreement to an end	7%	15%	23%	39%
Types of agreement used	7%	20%	22%	17%
Getting a grant for repairs or improvement	6%	16%	13%	31%
Taxation of rental income	8%	7%	10%	10%
Renewing a tenancy agreement	1%	6%	1%	11%
Base	91	81	78	81

Base: all landlords

11.9   The 1988 Housing Act attempted to resolve many of the difficulties which landlords face, for example by making it easier to regain possession, including cases where tenants were in arrears. It is noteworthy, therefore that a greater proportion of landlords letting on assured tenancies had difficulties dealing with arrears, difficult tenants and regaining possession than those who let on assured shorthold tenancies (Table 11.4).

Table 11.4 : Proportion of addresses whose landlords had problems since 1988 by type of agreement used at most recent letting

	Assured tenancy	Assured shorthold tenancy	Total (includes others)
Dealing with difficult tenants	78%	48%	44%
Dealing with rent arrears	65%	48%	43%
Regaining possession	56%	33%	33%
Bringing an agreement to an end	26%	23%	21%
Types of agreement used	9%	20%	16%
Renewing a tenancy agreement	13%	4%	5%
Base	23	188	331

Base: all landlords

11.10 Landlords who had experienced problems did not appear less likely to want to increase their lettings than those who had not had problems. For example, a quarter of the lettings whose owners had had arrears problems had landlords who expected their lettings to increase, compared with only 9% of those who had not experienced such problems (Table 11.5).

Table 11.5 : Proportion of addresses whose landlords had specific prblems since 1988 by whether landlords expected to increase lettings

		Expected change in lettings			
		Increase	Stay the same	Decrease	Base
Problems with difficult tenants					
Yes	%	24	50	23	145
No	%	10	68	19	186
Problems with arrears					
Yes	%	26	52	20	142
No	%	9	66	21	189
Problems with regaining possession					
Yes	%	31	48	23	103
No	%	10	65	20	228
Base: all landlords					

Advice about problems

11.11 If landlords and agents had experienced problems they were asked if they had sought advice about them (from someone outside their organisation, where they were not a private individual), from whom the advice had been sought, and whether or not they had found the advice helpful. Their responses showed that the great majority of landlords and agents had sought advice about most types of problems, that solicitors were predominantly the main source of the advice which had been sought and that the advice tendered had been found helpful in the great majority of cases (Table 11.6).

Table 11.6 : Proportion of addresses whose landlords and agents had problems who sought advice about those problems

	Landlord/ agent	% who sought advice about problem	% who sought advice from solicitor	% who found advice helpful
Dealing with difficult tenants:	Landlord	66	71	76
	Agent	64	91	98
Dealing with rent arrears:	Landlord	59	85	73
	Agent	72	87	92
Regaining possession:	Landlord	88	89	68
	Agent	94	92	94
Bringing an agreement to an end:	Landlord	84	88	75
	Agent	97	92	94
Types of agreement used:	Landlord	88	76	74
	Agent	84	94	100
Getting a grant for repairs or improvement:	Landlord	53	-	39
	Agent	53	-	83
Taxation of rental income:	Landlord	90	85†	61
	Agent	59	74†	79
Renewing a tenancy agreement:	Landlord	87	86	93
	Agent	69	82	100

†Note: advice from accountants

Base: Landlords and agents who had problems

11.12 There were, however, important differences. There was a tendency for landlords and agents to seek advice for fewer of the problems which beset most of them, like arrears, and to seek it more for those problems which were experienced by only a smaller proportion of them and/or which were related to important legal technicalities, like the type of agreement to use.

11.13 Thus, over 80% of those who had problems related to tenancy agreements (the type to use, their renewal and termination and regaining possession) sought advice about dealing with them. In the great majority of cases the main source of advice came from solicitors and the advice (whatever the source) was found helpful by approximately three quarters of landlords and over 90% of agents (Table 11.6).

11.14 A smaller proportion of landlords and agents who had problems related to arrears, difficult tenants, repairs/improvement grants and taxation sought advice about these, compared with problems related to tenancy agreements, even though arrears and difficult tenants were the problems experienced by the greatest proportion of landlords and agents. They consulted solicitors about arrears and difficult tenants in a large majority of cases and the majority found the advice they received helpful, especially agents (Table 11.6). Whilst solicitors were the overwhelming source of advice for problems related to agreements, arrears and difficult tenants, this was not the case for the two remaining types of problems: grants and taxation. A wide range of individuals and organisations were consulted for advice about grants, including local authorities, with no single source of advice being used by anything other than a small minority. Landlords and agents mainly consulted accountants for advice on taxation matters. Advice about grants and taxation was considered to be unhelpful by a somewhat greater proportion of agents and (especially) landlords than the advice received about other problems (Table 11.6).

Table 11.7 : Proportion of addresses whose landlords sought advice about problem by size of lettings portfolio and type of landlord (business or sideline)

		Size of lettings portfolio		Type of landlord	
		Less than 8	8+	Business	Sideline
Dealing with difficult tenants:	Advice	53	72	62	67
	Help	52	84	88	68
Dealing with rent arrears:	Advice	55	61	52	61
	Help	65	76	100	75
Regaining possession:	Advice	73	92	84	88
	Help	50	73	87	62
Bringing an agreement to an end:	Advice	72	88	82	85
	Help	61	80	85	69
Types of agreement used:	Advice	91	87	80	91
	Help	65	81	87	72
Getting a grant for repairs or improvement:	Advice	50	52	69	47
	Help	44	37	44	35
Taxation of rental income:	Advice	92	87	50	90
	Help	75	50	71	66
Renewing a tenancy agreement:	Advice	66	100	50	86
	Help	100	90	100	100
Sample number:	Advice				
	Help				
Base: all landlords who had problems					

11.15 Greater proportions of landlords with larger rather than smaller portfolios had sought advice, and the larger landlords were also more likely than smaller landlords to have found the advice helpful. Similarly, greater proportions of sideline than of business landlords sought advice for the problems they experienced, but business landlords were more likely than sideline landlords have found it helpful (Table 11.7).

Asking tenants to leave and court action

11.16 Given the extent to which landlords and agents reported that they had experienced problems with arrears and with difficult tenants, it was not surprising to discover that the landlords of 47% of addresses and the agents of 90% had asked a tenant to leave on at least one occasion since 1988 (Table 11.8). Two in three of the landlords and eight in 10 of the agents who had done so, had last done this in either 1993 or 1994. Not surprisingly, a greater proportion of landlords with larger portfolios than smaller ones had asked tenants to leave. For example, 76% of addresses whose owners had 41 or more addresses had landlords who had done so, compared with only 13% of those with only one address.

Table 11.8 : Proportion of addresses whose landlords and agents had asked tenants to leave since 1988		
		Base
(a) Landlords	47%	331
Agents	90%	181
(b) Type of landlord:		
Business	62%	63
Sideline	42%	246
Institute	59%	22
(c) Size of landlord's letting portfolio:		
1	13%	91
2-7	38%	81
8-40	64%	78
41+	76%	81

Base: all landlords and agents

11.17 The reasons they had for asking tenants to leave are listed in Table 11.9. It shows that arrears was the main reason in over half the cases, although types of unacceptable tenant behaviour (involving damage, noise, violence or abusive behaviour or other troublesome behaviour) were also important reasons. In addition, tenants were asked to leave when agreements had expired, because employment had ceased with respect to tied accommodation or because landlords wanted repossession on other grounds.

Table 11.9 : Main reasons landlords and agetns had for asking tenant to leave (on last occasion) since 1988		
	% giving reason	
	Landlords	Agents
Arrears	51	61
Abuse/damage	16	16
Noise	15	13
Tied Accommodation	8	<1
Troublesome tenants : other factors	5	2
Violent or abusive behaviour	4	5
Illegal sub-letting	4	<1
Termination of agreement	4	6
Repossession	3	15
Drugs	2	1
Mental/emotional problems	2	-
Problems with children	1	-
Pets	<1	<1
Tenants unreasonable demands	<1	<1
Selling accommodation	<1	4
Nonpayment of Housing Benefit	<1	2
Other	2	1
Base	163	155

Base: all landlords and agents who asked tenants to leave

11.18 In a significant proportion of cases this had resulted in court action being taken. For example, 41% and 48% of the last occasions when, respectively, landlords and agents had asked tenants to leave, resulted in court action being taken. Moreover 11% of landlords and 34% of agents who had not taken court action to get tenants to leave had, nonetheless, taken court action on other occasions. As a result 34% of all addresses had landlords and 77% of all addresses had agents who had taken court action at some time since 1988. Court action was more likely to have been taken by business and institutional landlords and by those with larger portfolios than by others (Table 11.10). The main grounds for the court actions taken were rent arrears and the recovery of accommodation of the end of a tenancy.

		Landlords type					Size of lettings portfolio			
		Agent	Bus-iness	Side-line	Institu-tional	All	1	2-7	8-40	41+
(a)	Took court action asking tenants to leave									
	% of those who asked tenants to leave	48%	39%	43%	46%	41%	17%	23%	34%	60%
	% of total	43%	16%	27%	10%	19%	2%	9%	22%	46%
(b)	Proportion of those who took court action on other occasion (if did not take action at (a))	34%	8%	21%	8%	11%	1%	7%	12%	26%
(c)	Percentage of total taking court action on some occasion since 1988	77%	24%	48%	19%	30%	3%	16%	35%	72%

Table 11.10 : Proportion of addresses whose agents and landlords had taken court action since 1988

Base: all landlords and agents

12   Information needs

Summary

12.1   The main findings of this chapter are:

- the most widely used sources of general information are managing and estate agents, solicitors, reading the legislation itself and property journals;

- agents, landlords with large portfolios, sideline landlords with investment motives and business landlords use far more sources of information than other landlords;

- only a minority of landlords and agents agreed that it was hard to find out how the law affects landlords;

- landlords with the largest portfolios were least likely to agree that it was hard to find out how the law affected them.

Introduction

12.2   Landlords and agents need a lot of information about the legal and financial framework for letting accommodation. It is a complex business, where the law and finance often change. Landlords not only need to ensure that they are fully aware of this complexity but also ensure that they are able to keep fully up to date.

12.3   Yet very little is known about the sources of information landlords rely upon and whether they find it easy or not to find out about matters that affect them, especially how they are affected by the law.

12.4   To fill this important gap in knowledge, landlords and agents were asked in the recent lettings survey where they got their information from. They were also asked in both surveys whether they found it hard or not to establish how the law affected them.

Information sources

12.5   The last chapter showed whether landlords sought advice when confronted with specific problems since 1988. This chapter looks at all the sources landlords and agents used when getting hold of information in general about letting accommodation.

Table 12.1 : Sources of general information used by landlords and agents			
Sources	% of addresses whose landlords used source	% of addresses whose agents used source	All
Solicitors	37	51	42
Managing/estate agent	31	46	36
Reading legislation	24	55	35
Property journals	10	44	22
Newspapers	19	25	21
Other landlords	16	18	17
DoE information leaflets	7	19	12
Landlords' associations	6	18	10
Friends/relatives/colleagues	10	9	10
Local council leaflets	8	15	10
Accountants	9	8	9
Housing aid centres	4	8	5
CABs	4	4	4
Other	9	14	11
None	17	4	13
Base	331	181	512

Base: all landlords and agents

12.6   A very wide range of sources were used to secure this general information, although some sources were used by a greater proportion of landlords and agents than others (Table 12.1). In particular, over 42% of addresses had landlords and agents who got their information from solicitors, 36% from managing or estate agents and 35% from reading the legislation itself. Information gleaned from property journals (22%), newspapers (21%), and other landlords (17%), were of rather less importance, but were, nonetheless, used by the landlords and agents of about one in five of addresses. Rather fewer, about 10% of addresses, had owners and managers who used landlords' associations, relatives or colleagues, and DoE or local council information leaflets. Other sources were used by only a small proportion, including accountants (9%), voluntary or local authority housing aid centres (5%) and citizens' advice bureaux (4%). However, only 13% of the sample had landlords or agents who did not use any source at all (Table 12.1).

12.7   There were important differences in the extent to which landlords and agents used these different sources. In general, a greater proportion of addresses had agents who used the sources listed than did landlords (Table 12.1). Four sources were most widely used by agents. About half addresses had agents who read the legislation themselves (55%), used solicitors (51%), and got information from fellow agents (46%), whilst 44% got their information from property journals. About one in five got information from other landlords (18%), landlords' associations (18%), Department of the Environment leaflets (19%) and newspapers (25%). Only 4% of agents used no sources of information.

12.8   Whilst the sources that were most used by agents were also the ones most used by landlords, they were used by a far smaller proportion. Thus the landlords of only 37% of addresses, compared with the agents of 51% of addresses got information from solicitors. Similarly, whereas the agents of 55% and 44% of addresses got information from reading the legislation and from property journals respectively, the landlords of only 24% and 10% of addresses used these two respective sources (Table 12.1). Noticeably, the landlords of 10% of addresses got information from friends and relatives, with fewer proportions than this getting it from landlords' associations, official information leaflets, citizens' advice bureaux or from housing aid centres. Furthermore 17% of addresses had landlords who used no source of general information about letting at all (Table 12.1).

Table 12.2 : Number of sources of general information used by landlords and agents		
Sources	Addresses whose landlords used sources	Addresses whose agents used sources
	%	%
None	18	5
1	29	14
2	22	23
3	16	19
4 or more	15	39
Base	331	181
Base: landlords and agents		

12.9   Moreover, different types of landlords used these sources to different extents. Thus, 39% of addresses had who agents identified four or more of the sources of general information listed in Table 12.1, compared with the landlords of 15% of addresses (Table 12.2). The landlords of 29% of addresses (that is, landlords who were in the main managing those properties themselves) used only one source, compared with the agents of only 14% of addresses (Table 12.2). However, landlords with larger portfolios tended to use rather more sources than those with smaller ones. For example the landlords of 43% of addresses which were in a portfolio of more than 40 lettings used three or more sources, compared with 23% of addresses whose landlords owned only that sample address (Table 12.3). Nevertheless, one in five of the largest landlords had no source of information, almost the same proportion of those with only one letting (Table 12.3).

Table 12.3 : Number of sources of general information used by landlords by size of landlords' total lettings portfolio

Sources	Size of lettings portfolio			
	1	2-7	8-40	41+
	%	%	%	%
None	18	15	18	21
1	34	37	28	17
2	25	21	22	18
3	15	17	14	18
4 or more	8	10	18	25
Base	91	81	78	81

Base: all landlords

12.10 The type of landlord was also related to the number of sources of information. Institutional landlords were much more likely than others to use no sources at all (Table 12.4). Those who used the most sources were sideline landlords who regarded their most recent letting as an investment, the landlords of 36% of these addresses using three or more sources (Table 12.4).

Table 12.4 : Number of sources of general information used by landlords by landlord type

Sources	Type of landlord			
	Sideline sample letting		Business	Institutional
	Noninvestment	Investment		
	%	%	%	%
None	23	10	16	30
1	30	31	27	24
2	21	22	27	13
3	13	22	14	11
4 or more	12	14	16	22
Base	113	118	63	37

Base: all landlords

12.11 There were also significant variations in the specific sources used by different landlords. Landlords with larger portfolios were more likely than those with smaller ones to get information from landlords' associations, Department of the Environment and local authority leaflets, property journals and from reading the legislation (Table 12.5). Landlords with smaller portfolios were more likely than those with larger ones to get their information from accountants, friends and relatives, and citizens' advice bureaux (Table 12.5). Sideline landlords were more likely to get information from accountants and friends and relatives than business and institutional landlords. Business and institutional landlords were more likely than others to use landlords' associations, property journals and reading the legislation (Table 12.6).

Table 12.5 : Sources of general information used by landlords by size of landlords' total lettings portfolio				
Sources	% of addresses whose landlords used source			
	Size of lettings portfolio			
	1	2-7	8-40	41+
Solicitors	35	41	33	41
Managing/estate agents	33	26	37	30
Reading legislation	8	17	27	44
Property journals	1	-	14	27
Newspapers	22	22	17	16
Other landlords	9	21	19	17
DoE information leaflets	3	5	8	14
Landlords' associations	2	3	6	12
Friends/relatives/colleagues	20	12	8	-
Local council leaflets	7	5	5	15
Accountants	13	12	9	2
Housing aid centres	2	1	6	5
CABs	12	3	1	1
Other	1	10	9	16
None	18	15	17	21
Sample number	91	81	78	81
Base: all landlords				

Table 12.6 : Sources of general information used by landlords by landlord type

Sources	Type of landlord			
	Sideline sample letting		Business	Institutional
	Non-investment	Investment		
	%	%	%	%
Solicitors	34	38	38	43
Managing/estate agents	30	35	27	32
Reading legislation	14	23	36	32
Property journals	6	5	22	19
Newspapers	15	28	19	5
Other landlords	12	21	21	5
DoE information leaflets	5	8	5	13
Landlords' association	3	3	16	5
Friends/relatives/colleagues	19	7	8	-
Local council leaflets	7	9	5	11
Accountants	9	14	5	5
Housing aid centres	1	5	3	8
CABs	9	2	2	3
Other	4	13	6	13
None	23	10	14	30
Base	113	118	63	37

Base: all landlords

Finding out how the law affects landlords

12.12 Based upon their own experience, the landlords of a third (33%) of addresses and the agents of a fifth (22%) agreed or strongly agreed with the statement that *it is hard for landlords to find out how they are affected by the law* (Table 12.7). However, a larger proportion of both landlords and agents disagreed. The landlords of 44% of addresses and the agents of 66% of addresses said they disagreed with the statement. Thus, whilst there is a wide spread of experience about this, only a minority of the sample had landlords and agents who agree that it is hard for them to find out how the law affected them (Table 12.7).

Table 12.7 : Landlords' and agents' views on whether it is hard for landlords to find out how they are affected by the law

View	Addresses whose landlords held view	Address whose agents held view
	%	%
Strongly agree	5	2
Agree	28	20
Neither agree nor disagree	12	10
Disagree	41	60
Strongly disagree	3	6
Don't know/NA	11	2
Base	543	270

Base: all landlords and agents

12.13 Not only were landlords with the largest portfolios more likely than those with smaller ones to disagree with the statement, but landlords with few lettings were more likely than those with many lettings to have been unable to offer an opinion (Table 12.8). Thus, larger landlords were most likely to feel informed about the law. Table 12.9 shows that it was institutional landlords who were least likely to agree with the statement (and also to have no opinion), compared with other types of landlord.

Table 12.8 : Landlords' views on whether it is hard for landlords to find out how they are affected by the law by size of landlords' total lettings portfolio

View	Total in lettings portfolio			
	1	2-7	8-40	41+
	%	%	%	%
Strongly agree	4	4	6	4
Agree	27	37	38	13
Neither agree nor disagree	20	8	9	10
Disagree	29	37	40	58
Strongly disagree	1	-	3	6
Don't know/NA	18	14	3	9
Base	138	132	123	150

Base: all landlords

Table 12.9 : Landlords' views on whether it is hard for landlords to find out how they are affected by the law by type of landlord

Sources	Type of landlord			
	Sideline sample letting		Business	Institutional
	Non-investment	Investment		
	%	%	%	%
Strongly agree	2	8	4	3
Agree	25	34	34	14
Neither agree nor disagree	16	9	9	10
Disagree	40	40	46	44
Strongly disagree	2	1	3	10
Don't know/NA	15	8	5	19
Base:	197	184	103	59

Base: all landlords

12.14 Not surprisingly, perhaps, the more sources of information landlords and agents used to get general information about letting accommodation, the more likely they were to disagree that it was hard to find out how the law affected them. Thus 55% of addresses whose landlords used four or more sources had landlords who disagreed, compared with 30% whose owners had no sources of general information (Table 12.10).

Table 12.10 : Landlords' views on whether it is hard for landlords to find out how they are affected by the law by number of information sources used for general information

View	Number of sources of general information				
	None	1	2	3	4+
	%	%	%	%	%
Strongly agree	-	4	11	6	10
Agree	29	29	29	35	24
Neither agree nor disagree	14	16	14	7	8
Disagree	25	39	36	46	51
Strongly disagree	5	1	1	4	4
Don't know/NA	27	10	8	2	2
Base	59	97	72	54	49

Base: all landlords

12.15 Detailed analysis showed that those landlords who used citizens' advice bureaux and housing aid centres for their general information were statistically more likely to agree that it was hard to find out how the law affected them than those who did not use these sources. Those who got their general information from managing or estate agents, solicitors, and property journals were more likely to disagree that it was hard to find out than those who did not use these sources (Table 12.11).

Table 12.11 : Landlords' views on whether it is hard for landlords to find out how they are affected by the law by types of information source used for general information

Sources	View of those using specific source listed						
	Strongly agree	Agree	Neither agree nor Disagree	Disagree	Strongly disagree	Don't know/ NA	Base
	%	%	%	%	%	%	%
Solicitors	6	29	11	47	2	4	124
Managing/estate agent	6	22	14	50	2	6	104
Reading legislation	5	32	8	49	4	3	78
Property journals	9	23	9	47	12	-	34
Newspapers	8	31	9	37	5	9	64
Other landlords	9	35	9	39	2	6	54
DoE information leaflets	17	29	4	46	4	-	24
landlords' associations	16	37	-	42	5	-	19
Friends/relatives/ colleagues	12	38	12	23	-	15	34
Local council leaflets	11	27	8	54	-	-	26
Accountants	13	23	10	45	3	6	31
Housing aid centres	33	25	8	33	-	-	12
CABs	33	20	13	33	-	-	15
Other	14	28	10	41	3	3	29
None	-	28	14	26	5	27	58
All landlords	6	29	13	39	3	10	331

Base: all landlords

13   Future intentions

Summary

- the majority of privately rented addresses would be relet if they became vacant tomorrow; properties let after 1988 were more likely to be relet than those let prior to that date;

- a great variety of reasons was given by landlords as to why they would not relet accommodation that became vacant; in only a minority of cases was it due to insufficient financial returns or the hassles of letting accommodation; many of the reasons given were related to their personal circumstances and were noneconomic. This reflected the variety of reasons why landlords had been letting the accommodation in the first place;

- the majority of privately rented addresses were owned by landlords who did not expect the size of their lettings portfolio to change in the next two years; among those who thought it would change, more thought it would increase than thought it would decrease, though the difference was not very large;

- three out of five landlords said that they would not expect to adjust the size of their lettings portfolio in response to three specified changes in rents and house prices;

- the scenario most likely to produce an *expansion* of portfolios was if rents were to increase each year but house prices remain the same; the scenario most likely to produce a *contraction* of portfolios was if rents were to stay the same each year but house prices increase;

- business landlords, investment motivated landlords (income seekers more than growth seekers), landlords for whom rent accounted for more than a quarter of their income, and larger landlords, were the most likely to say (i) they would relet their accommodation if it became vacant, (ii) they expected to increase the number of lettings they had in the next two years, (iii) would want to increase their portfolio in response to specified changes in rents and house prices;

Introduction   13.1   This chapter examines three key questions which shed light on the future prospects for the privately rented sector from the perspective of the suppliers of accommodation. First, what landlords would do if the letting became vacant: would they relet the accommodation, occupy it themselves or sell it? Second, whether landlords expected the number of lettings they had to increase, decrease or remain the same in the next two years. Third, whether landlords would want adjust the number of lettings they had in response to changes in rents and in house prices

Reletting vacancies

13.2   An important indicator of the immediate prospects for the privately rented sector is what landlords would do if a letting in their portfolio were to become vacant. If a high proportion of landlords intend to relet their vacancies then this suggests, if not confidence in the market, then at worst that the sector is unlikely to shrink much in size in the short term. If, on the other hand, a high proportion of landlords intend not to relet vacancies then this could suggest that the sector is likely to decline and could reflect a lack of confidence in the lettings market.

13.3   Landlords were therefore asked what they would do with a vacancy. Where the address was let to one tenant, landlords were asked what they would do if it became vacant tomorrow or what they expected to do if it was already vacant. If the address was let to more than one tenant, landlords were asked what they would do if all of the lettings at the address became vacant or were already vacant.

13.4   As Table 13.1 shows, in both samples the majority of addresses which were let to one tenant had landlords that said they would relet the accommodation[†]. Thus in the all lettings sample, 62% of addresses had landlords who said they would relet a vacancy, while a further 6% said they would improve or convert the accommodation and the relet it; in the recent lettings samples, 69% would relet and a further 5% would improve or convert the accommodation prior to reletting it. The next most commonly expected action in response to a vacancy - mentioned by landlords at 19% of addresses in the all lettings sample and 17% in the recent lettings sample - was to sell the accommodation; a further 2% in the all lettings sample said they would improve or convert the accommodation prior to resale. In both samples, landlords at 2% of addresses said they would occupy it themselves in the event of a vacancy, while 7% and 4% respectively said they would leave it empty for the time being. The pattern of responses was very similar where the address was let to more than one tenant (compare Table 13.1 with 13.2).

---

† The differences between the two samples were not statistically significant; in other words, they could have been due to chance rather than reflecting a real difference in expectations.

Table 13.1 : What landlords would expect to do if the letting became vacant tomorrow

	All lettings	Recent lettings
	%	%
Let it	62	69
Improve or convert it to let	6	5
Sell it	19	17
Improve or convert it to sell	2	0
Occupy it	2	2
Leave it empty for now	7	4
Something else/not applicable	3	3
Total	**100**	**100**
(Base)	(183)	(254)

Base: addresses let to one tenant

Table 13.2 : What landlords would expect to do if all of the lettings at the addresses became vacant tomorrow

	All lettings	Recent lettings
	%	%
Let them	59	66
Improve or convert them to let	3	3
Sell them	21	22
Improve or convert them to sell	3	1
Occupy them	0	1
Leave them empty for now	7	4
Something else/not applicable	7	3
Total	100	100
(Base)	(29)	(77)

Base: addresses let to more than one tenant

13.5   Table 13.3 shows what the different types of landlord in each of the two samples would do if the letting (at addresses let to one tenant) were to become vacant tomorrow. Although the pattern of responses within the two samples was similar, the differences were not quite statistically significant in the all lettings sample but were so in the recent lettings sample. The majority of lettings owned by business, institutional and sideline investment landlords would be relet if they were to become vacant, but only about half of those owned by sideline

170

noninvestment landlords would be. Lettings owned by sideline noninvestment landlords were much more likely that those owned by other types of landlord to be sold or left empty if they were to become vacant.

Table 13.3 : What landlords would do if the letting became vacant tomorrow, by type of landlord							
	All lettings				Recent lettings		
	Business	Sideline		Institution	Business	Sideline	Institution
		Investment	Non-investment				
	%	%	%	%	%	%	%
Let it	78	67	49	67	88	62	80
Sell it	14	18	23	11	12	20	7
Other	8	15	28	22	-	18	13
Total	100	100	100	100	100	100	100
(Base)	(36)	(55)	(74)	(18)	(41)	(182)	(30)

Base: addresses let to one tenant

13.6   Again, in both samples, addresses let by income seekers were much more likely to be relet if the accommodation became vacant than those let by growth seekers and, to a lesser extent, by other types of landlord. Addresses let by growth seeker landlords were more likely to be sold if a vacancy arose than those let by income seekers and employer landlords (Table 13.4).

Table 13.4 : What landlords would do if the letting became vacant tomorrow							
	All lettings				Recent lettings		
	Growth seeker	Income seeker	Employer	Other	Growth seeker	Income seeker	Employer	Other
	%	%	%	%	%	%	%	%
Let it	49	92	63	48	58	86	79	52
Sell it	24	9	13	25	32	8	0	27
Other	27	0	23	28	11	6	21	22
Total	100	100	100	100	100	100	100	100
(Base)	(41)	(47)	(30)	(65)	(38)	(88)	(33)	(93)

Base: addresses where the landlord was interviewed

13.7   Addresses where the most recent tenancy began after the implementation of the deregulation provisions of the 1988 Housing Act were more likely to be relet than those where the most recent tenancy was taken out before deregulation in January 1989. This was true of both samples, but particularly of the recent lettings sample (Table 13.5).

Table 13.5 : What landlords would do if the letting became vacant tomorrow, by date of most recent tenancy

	All lettings		Recent lettings	
	Before 15 January 1989	After 15 January 1989	Before 15 January 1989	After 15 January 1989
Let it	52	70	28	76
Sell it	25	13	36	14
Other	23	17	36	10
Total	100	100	100	100
(Base)	(83)	(100)	(39)	(215)

Base: addresses let to one tenant

13.8   Also in both samples, dividing lettings portfolios in quartiles, landlords with larger letting portfolios were more likely to indicate that they would relet a vacancy than those with only one or a few lettings. Thus, in the recent lettings sample, only 49% of addresses held by landlords with only one letting said they would relet a vacancy, compared with 53% owned by those with between two and seven lettings, 65% of those owned by landlords with from eight to 40 lettings, and 78% by those with 41 or more lettings. Likewise, in the recent lettings sample, the respective percentages of expected reletting were 45%, 69%, 83% and 90%. Correspondingly, addresses owned by smaller scale landlords were more likely than was the case with large scale landlords to be sold if a vacancy arose.

13.9   Similarly, in both samples, addresses owned by landlords for whom rent from residential lettings accounted for more than a quarter of their income were statistically much more likely to say that they would relet a vacancy than those for whom it represented a quarter or less of their income. Thus in the all lettings sample, 84% of addresses held by landlords for whom residential rent accounted for more than a quarter of their income would be relet if a vacancy occurred, compared with 56% where rent accounted for a quarter or less of their income; in the recent lettings sample were 88% and 59% respectively said they would relet the accommodation.

Table 13.6 : Gross estimated rental yield by what the landlord would do if the letting became vacant		
	All lettings	Recent lettings
	%	%
Let it	6.3	7.7
Sell it	5.3	6.3
Other	4.0	4.4
(Base)	(164)	(210)

Base: addresses that had been purchased, where rent was charged and which were let to one tenant

13.10 It might be expected that landlords' reletting intentions would relate to the profitability of the letting. However, as discussed in Chapter 5, many landlords were not primarily, or even at all, letting accommodation for investment reasons. In fact, estimated gross rental yields were about one % higher for addresses where the landlord said they would relet the accommodation compared with those where they said they would sell it (Table 13.6).

13.11 The main reason given by landlords as to why they would not relet the accommodation if it became vacant was that they wanted to release the money to spend it on other things; this was mentioned by landlords at 23% of addresses in the all lettings sample where the landlord would not relet and 39% in the recent lettings sample. The next most commonly mentioned reasons were that it was not financially viable to let their accommodation or cost too much to do so (21% and 14%); and that they wanted to keep it available for someone, either themselves, a member of their family or other relative, or a friend. Bad experiences with letting the accommodation were mentioned by the landlords of three times as many addresses in the all lettings sample as in the recent lettings sample (18% compared with six %). A number of landlords mentioned that there would be no need to relet the accommodation if it became vacant because they were only letting it in order to help out a particular person (such as a friend, a relative or an employee). Finally, some landlords said that letting accommodation was too much responsibility and that was why they would not relet a vacancy (nine % in both samples). A miscellany of other reasons were mentioned as to why they would not relet the accommodation if it became vacant.

13.12 Thus landlords gave a variety of reasons for not wanting to relet accommodation that became vacant. In only a minority of cases was this due to a perceived inadequate return from letting accommodation or because of the troubles and anxieties of doing so. Very often it related to their noneconomic motives for letting the accommodation in the first place, the rationale for which no longer applied.

**Portfolio
expectations**

13.13 Landlords do not necessarily have to wait for their accommodation to become vacant in order to dispose of it, though as discussed in Chapter 7, they will get substantially less for it if they sell with sitting tenants. At the same time, ascertaining what might happen if one of their existing lettings becomes vacant does not necessarily tell us (in the case of landlords with more than one letting) what they would do if they all became vacant. Nor does it tell us about whether they would invest in new lettings, either to replace any that are sold or in addition to those they already own. Landlords were therefore asked whether the total number of lettings they had was likely to increase, decrease, or remain about the same in the next two years.

13.14 As Table 13.7 shows, the majority of addresses were held by landlords who did not expect the size of their letting portfolio to change over the next two years. Among addresses held by landlords who did expect their portfolio to change, more thought that it would decrease than thought it would get bigger. Thus three fifths of addresses were owned by landlords who said the number of their lettings would be the same, while a quarter were owned by landlords who said they would reduce their portfolio and a sixth said it would increase in size.

Table 13.7 : Whether landlords thought the number of their lettings would increase, decrease or remain about the same in the next two years

	%
Increase	17
Decrease	24
Remain the same	59
Total	100
(Base)	(526)

Base: addresses where landlords were interviewed

13.15 Respondents at addresses owned by both business and sideline investment landlords were much more likely than those at addresses owned by sideline noninvestment landlords to say that their portfolio was likely to increase in size and less likely to say it would decrease in size; the proportion saying it would remain unchanged was similar. Addresses owned by institutional landlords, however, were the most likely to have landlords who said that their portfolio would increase and the least likely to say it would remain unchanged (Table 13.8).

	Business	Sideline		Institution
		Investment	Noninvestment	
	%	%	%	%
Increase	20	20	8	33
Decrease	19	16	33	26
Remain the same	61	64	60	41
Total	**100**	**100**	**100**	**100**
(Base)	(101)	(178)	(187)	(58)

Base: addresses where landlords were interviewed

13.16 Looking at how landlords regarded the address, those held by landlords who saw the it as a source of rental income were more likely than those who saw it as a source of capital gain (26% compared with 12%) to have a respondent who said that their portfolio would increase and less likely to say it would decrease (14% compared with 25%). A greater proportion of addresses held by employers had landlords who said their portfolio would decrease (30%) than said it would increase (18%). Addresses owned by slump landlords were much more likely to have respondents who said the number of lettings they had would decrease than said it would increase (30% compared with 9%); but the majority said it would remain the same (61%), which suggests that they were not optimistic about the short term projects for turnover or prices in the owner occupied housing market[†].

13.17 When portfolio size is divided up into quartiles, the propensity to say that the number of lettings would increase over the next two years increased as portfolio size increased. Thus only 4% of respondents at addresses owned by landlords with one letting said their portfolio would increase in the next two years, compared with 14% among those with between two and seven lettings, 23% among those with eight to 40 lettings, and 28% among those with 41 or more lettings. The propensity to say that the number of lettings would remain unchanged fell as portfolio size increased, with landlords owning just one letting being the most likely to say their portfolio would not change and those with 41 or more lettings being the least likely to give that response. However, there appeared to be no relationship between portfolio size and whether the number of lettings owned was expected to decrease in size over the next two years (Table 13.9).

† However, the sample number of slump landlord addresses for this question is small and therefore is subject to a large margin of error.

Table 13.9 : Whether landlords thought the number of their lettings would increase, decrease or remain about the same in the next two years, by size of portfolio				
	1 letting	2 to 7 lettings	8 to 40 lettings	41 + lettings
	%	%	%	%
Increase	4	14	23	28
Decrease	24	18	20	30
Remain the same	73	68	57	42
Total	**100**	**100**	**100**	**100**
(Base)	(136)	(126)	(119)	(125)
Base: addresses where landlords were interviewed				

13.18 Interviewees at addresses held by landlords for whom residential rent accounted for more than a quarter of their income were significantly more likely than those for whom it represented up to a quarter of their income, to say that they expected to increase the size of their portfolio (27% compared with 13%); and, conversely, were less likely to say it would decrease in size (17% compared with 27%).

13.19 Landlords who said that the rent *from the address* was sufficient were more likely than those who said it was insufficient to say their portfolio would increase and less likely to say it would decrease; the proportion would said it would remain unchanged was similar. Thus landlords at 22% of addresses where the rent was felt to be sufficient said they would increase the number of lettings they had, whereas only 11% said the same where the rent was considered to be insufficient. Where the rent for the address was considered to be sufficient, 20% said they would reduce their portfolio, compared with 27% where the rent was regarded as insufficient.

13.20 Expectations about whether the number of lettings which landlords had would change over the next two years were also examined by whether or not the rental income *from their portfolio as a whole* was considered to be sufficient to cover all necessary repairs and give a reasonable return. The results, which are shown in Table 13.10, clearly indicate that landlords who thought their portfolio return was reasonable were more likely than those who though it was not reasonable, to say that the total number of lettings they had would increase and less likely to say it would decrease. Compared with those who did want a return, a much higher proportion of addresses where the landlord said they did not was a return had respondents who did not expect to alter the size of their portfolio over the next two years (Table 13.10).

Table 13.10 : Whether landlords thought the number of their lettings would increase, decrease or remain about the same in the next two years, by whether they thought their rental income was sufficient to cover all necessary repairs and give a reasonable return

	Reasonable	Not reasonable	Don't want a return	Other
	%	%	%	%
Increase	26	8	13	38
Decrease	15	35	17	6
Remain the same	59	57	70	56
Total	**100**	**100**	**100**	**100**
(Base)	(227)	(223)	(54)	(16)

13.21   There were statistically significant differences, about whether the landlord's portfolio size would increase, decrease or remain the same in the next two years, between landlords according to whether they agreed or disagreed with the statement that *"Landlords only let if they can't sell"*. Among addresses where the landlord agreed with this statement, only five per cent of respondents said their portfolio would increase, while 45% said it would decrease. Among addresses where the landlord said they disagreed with the statement, there was little difference between those who said it would go up and those who thought it would go down (Table 13.11).

Table 13.11 : Whether landlords thought the number of their lettings would increase, decrease or remain the same in the next two years, by whether they agreed that "landlords only let if they can't sell"

	Landlords only let if they can't sell		
	Agree	Neither agree nor disagree	Disagree
	%	%	%
Increase	5	14	20
Decrease	45	26	18
Remain the same	51	60	62
Total	**100**	**100**	**100**
(Base)	(83)	(87)	(347)

Base: addresses where landlords were interviewed

13.22   In the recent lettings sample, and to a much lesser extent in the all lettings sample, the gross rental yield was higher among addresses where the landlord said their portfolio would increase than among those where they said it would decrease (Table 13.12).

Table 13.12 : Gross estimated rental yield by whether the landlord thought the number of their lettings would increase, decrease or remain about the same in the next two years

	All lettings	Recent lettings
	%	%
Increase	7.1	11.0
Decrease	6.3	8.1
Remain the same	5.5	7.2
(Base)	(180)	(273)

Base: addresses at which rent was being charged

Likely responses to rent and house price changes

13.23 The future prospects of the privately rented sector, on both the supply and the demand side, are likely to be significantly affected by what happens to rents and house prices. In order to ascertain how investment sensitive landlords are to changes in house prices and in rents, they were asked what they would do in three different rent and house prices scenarios (see Table 13.13).

Table 13.13 : How landlords thought they might respond to changes in rents and house prices

	(a) Rents increase each year but house prices stay the same	(b) Rents stay the same but house prices increase	(c) Both rents and house prices increase each year
	%	%	%
Definitely increase	10	4	8
Possibly increase	20	8	15
Remain the same	52	51	54
Possibly reduce	3	14	7
Definitely reduce	3	10	4
Not applicable	11	10	11
Don't know	2	2	2
Total	**100**	**100**	**100**
(Base)	(539)	(539)	(539)

Base: addresses where landlords were interviewed

13.24   The first scenario was that *Rents increase each year but house prices remain the same*. The results are set out in Table 13.13. This shows that, if rents were to increase each year while house prices remained the same, three out of 10 privately rented addresses had landlords who said that they would either definitely or possibly want to increase their lettings; half had landlords who would not want to change their portfolio size; and only about one in 20 had landlords that would want to decrease their holdings.

13.25   The second scenario was that *Rents stay the same each year but house prices increase* (Table 13.13). For this scenario, one in eight addresses had landlords that would want to increase their portfolio, while a quarter would want to decrease it. Half of all addresses again had landlords who would want neither to increase nor to decrease the size of their portfolio but rather keep it the same.

13.26   The third scenario was that *Both rents and house prices increase each year* (Table 13.14c), in which case rental yields would remain unchanged but there would be capital appreciation. Landlords at about a quarter of addresses said that, in these circumstances, they would want to increase their portfolio, while about one in 10 would want to reduce it, and just over half would want it to remain unchanged.

13.27   Thus the scenario most likely to result in expansion among existing suppliers was (a) - rents increase in year but house prices remain the same - in which circumstances rental yields would increase but there would be no capital gain. The one most likely to produce a contraction of existing supply was scenario (b) - rents stay the same each year but house prices increase - in which circumstances landlords would benefit from capital appreciation, but rental yields would get progressively lower.

13.28   However, the most common response to all three scenarios was neither increase nor decrease but rather no change in portfolio size: in all cases, about a half of addresses had landlords who gave this response. In addition, in all three scenarios, about one in ten addresses had landlords who said that the question was just not applicable to them. Thus, in total, about three out of five landlords were unlikely to adjust their letting portfolio in response changes in the two variables which affect the investment returns from house property. This once again emphasises the noninvestment orientation of many landlords.

	Business	Sideline		Institution
		Investment	Noninvestment	
	%	%	%	%
Increase	48	35	22	12
Stay the same	47	59	52	42
Reduce	4	3	10	2
Not applicable	2	3	16	44
Total	**100**	**100**	**100**	**100**
(Base)	(101)	(183)	(195)	(57)

Base: addresses where landlords were interviewed

Table 13.14b : Whether landlords thought the number of properties they would like to let would increase, reduce or stay the same if *rents stay the same each year but house prices increase*, by type of landlord

	Business	Sideline		Institution
		Invest ment	Noninvestment	
	%	%	%	%
Increase	16	18	5	7
Stay the same	50	59	50	39
Reduce	32	19	28	11
Not applicable	2	5	17	44
Total	**100**	**100**	**100**	**100**
(Base)	(100)	(183)	(195)	(57)

Base: addresses where landlords were interviewed

	Business	Sideline		Institution
		Investment	Noninvestment	
	%	%	%	%
Increase	30	31	13	9
Stay the same	58	56	54	45
Reduce	10	8	16	4
Not applicable	2	5	17	43
Total	**100**	**100**	**100**	**100**
(Base)	(100)	(183)	(195)	(56)

Table 13.14c : Whether landlords thought the number of properties they would like to let would increase, reduce or stay the same if *both rents and house prices increase each year*, by type of landlord

Base: addresses where landlords were interviewed

13.29 Nevertheless, some landlords were more responsive than others to changes in rents and house prices. As Table 13.14a shows, if scenario (a) were to develop - that is, rents increase each year but house prices remain the same - addresses held by business landlords and, to a lesser extent, by sideline investment landlords were much more likely than sideline noninvestment and institutional landlords to say that they would want to expand their portfolios. In scenario (b) - rents stay the same each year but house prices increase - business and sideline investment landlords were more likely than sideline noninvestment or institutional landlords to say that they would want to contract their portfolio (Table 13.14b). And in scenario (c) - both rents and house prices increase each year - business landlords and sideline investment landlords were again more likely than the other types of landlord to say their would want to increase the number of lettings they had (Table 13.14c).

13.30 In all three scenarios, just over two fifths of addresses held by institutional landlords and about a sixth held by sideline noninvestment landlords had respondents who said that the question of changing their lettings in response to developments in house prices and rents was not applicable to them; in contrast, relatively few addresses had sideline investment or business landlords who said this.

Table 13.15a : Whether landlords thought the number of properties they would like to let would increase, reduce or stay the same if *rents increase each year but house prices stay the same*, by whether they thought their rental income was sufficient to cover all necessary repairs and give a reasonable return

	Reasonable	Not reasonable	Don't want a return	Other
	%	%	%	%
Increase	39	28	10	31
Stay the same	53	57	40	25
Reduce	3	10	2	0
Not applicable	5	5	48	43
Total	**100**	**100**	**100**	**100**
(Base)	(227)	(229)	(52)	(16)

Base: addresses where landlords were interviewed

13.31 Tables 13.15a to 13.15c show landlord responses to the rent and house price scenario questions according to whether they thought the rental income from all of their lettings was sufficient to cover all necessary repairs and give a reasonable return. In all three scenarios, nearly half of respondents of addresses where the landlord did not want a return said that the question was not applicable to them. Among addresses where the rental income was thought to be reasonable, two fifths said that, in scenario (a), they would want to increase their portfolio, compared with three tenths of addresses where the landlord said the return on the portfolio was not considered to be reasonable (Table 13.15a). In scenario (b) a third of respondents at addresses where the landlord thought the portfolio return was not reasonable said that they would contract their lettings, compared with a fifth among addresses where the return was thought to be reasonable (Table 13.15b). In scenario (c), respondents at addresses were the landlord thought the return was reasonable were more likely than those who thought it was not reasonable, to say that they would increase their lettings and less likely to say they would reduce them (Table 13.15c).

Table 13.15b : Whether landlords thought the number of properties they would like to let would increase, reduce or stay the same if *rents stay the same each year but house prices increase*, by whether they thought their rental income was sufficient to cover all necessary repairs and give a reasonable return

	Reasonable	Not reasonable	Don't want a return	Other
	%	%	%	%
Increase	19	7	4	19
Stay the same	55	55	42	31
Reduce	20	33	6	6
Not applicable	5	5	48	44
Total	**100**	**100**	**100**	**100**
(Base)	(223)	(229)	(52)	(16)

Base: addresses where landlords were interviewed

Table 13.15c : Whether landlords thought the number of properties they would like to let would increase, reduce or stay the same if *both rents and house prices increase each year*, by whether they thought their rental income was sufficient to cover all necessary repairs and give a reasonable return

	Reasonable	Not reasonable	Don't want a return	Other
	%	%	%	%
Increase	32	18	10	19
Stay the same	55	61	40	31
Reduce	8	16	2	6
Not applicable	5	5	48	44
Total	**100**	**100**	**100**	**100**
(Base)	(224)	(227)	(52)	(16)

Base: addresses where landlords were interviewed

14 Views on policy

Summary

14.1   The main findings of this chapter are that:

- half the lettings that landlords did not expect to relet had owners who said that there were no changes that would persuade them to relet instead;

- a quarter of landlords and half agents said that getting easier repossession or having less troublesome tenants was the one change that would most help landlords;

- more landlords said that paying less tax would be of most help than those who said that higher rents would help most;

- few landlords said that government subsidies and grants would help most, but those that did were more likely to say that they expected their portfolio to increase in size;

- individual landlords said that paying less tax would be the most helpful form of financial assistance from the government; company landlords were more likely than individual landlords to select other forms of assistance, including grants and capital allowances;

- landlords who expected their total lettings to increase were more likely than others to have said that grants would be the most helpful form of financial assistance from the government.

Introduction

14.2   If the continued expansion of a viable private rented sector requires changes to policy, it is important to know what kinds of changes landlords think would help them the most. Given the variety that exists in the types of landlords, their reasons for being landlords and the way they regard their lettings, it is also important to know how, if at all, preferred changes vary according to different types of landlords.

14.3   In order to find out what changes would be welcomed, landlords and their agents were asked about what, if any, changes they wanted. The chapter examines the changes that landlords and agents said would most help individuals and companies (and other organisations). It describes their views on three issues:

- the changes that would persuade landlords to relet the sample lettings which they said they did not intend to let if they became vacant;

- the changes that would most help all landlords;

- the type of financial assistance from the Government that would most help individual and company landlords.

Changes that would persuade landlords to relet

14.4   As Chapter 11 showed, most lettings (68% of all lettings and 74% of recent lettings) would be relet if they became vacant. In the minority of cases where landlords did not expect to relet, they were asked what changes would be sufficient to persuade them to relet instead. As Table 14.1 shows, almost half of all lettings (45%) and of recent lettings (48%) which would not be relet, had landlords who said that no changes would be sufficient to persuade them. These can be regarded as a small core of lettings which will disappear from the private rented sector, irrespective of government policy or of other changes.

Table 14.1 : The changes that would be sufficient to persuade landlords to relet accommodation		
	All lettings	Recent lettings
Higher rents	21%	23%
Easier repossession	17%	10%
Less tax on rent income	17%	23%
Less troublesome tenants	14%	15%
Falling house prices	14%	23%
Less tax on capital gain	4%	11%
Less building control/environmental health regulation	-	6%
Something else	8%	1%
None	45%	48%
Can't say	-	-
Not applicable	19%	14%
Base	66	87

Base: all landlords who said they would not relet

14.5   Fourteen % of all lettings and 23% of recent lettings which were not to be relet, had landlords who would, however, relet if house prices kept on falling. Thus, a small proportion of the private rented sector (approximately 4.5% of all lettings) is likely to be retained if prices continue to fall.

14.6   Factors related to the legal framework and its operation and factors related to the types of tenants could influence some landlords to relet instead. Having easier repossession and less troublesome tenants would, for example, persuade the landlords of 17% and 14%, respectively, of all lettings to relet.

14.7   In addition the level of rents which can be charged and the tax paid on net rent income are other factors which would influence some landlords to relet. Thus nearly a quarter of recent lettings (23%) had landlords who said that higher rents and having to pay less tax on rental income would be sufficient to persuade them to relet.

14.8   Having to pay less tax on capital gains or having to comply with fewer environmental health and building regulations would be changes which would be sufficient to persuade the landlords of much smaller proportions of lettings to relet.

The changes that would most help landlords

14.9   To understand landlords' motives and aspirations more fully, landlords and agents were asked about legislative and fiscal changes which some commentators have proposed. Landlords were asked what would be the one change that would most help them as landlords. Agents were asked what would be the change that would most help landlords.   Table 14.2 lists the changes from which landlords and agents were asked to select. It will be noted that only a small proportion identified something that was not on the list shown to them.

Table 14.2 : The change that would most help landlords according to landlords and agents	Landlords	Agents
	%	%
Less tax on rent income	22	23
Higher rents	17	12
Easier repossession	17	30
Government subsidies or grant	10	7
Less troublesome tenants	8	16
Less tax on capital gain	6	3
Less building control/environmental health regulation	3	1
A better public image	2	4
Something else	2	4
None	11	1
Not applicable	1	<1
Base	543	270
Base: all landlords and agents		

14.10   Seventeen % of lettings had landlords who said that getting easier repossession of their accommodation would be the most help. Landlords who selected this change were much more likely than others to have had problems letting accommodation since 1988. In particular 32% of the lettings whose landlords had problems regaining possession since 1988 had landlords who selected easier repossession as the most helpful change. In comparison, only 9% of lettings whose landlords said they had not had problems with repossession had owners who picked out easier repossession as the change they wanted. However, the overall proportion of 17% lettings whose landlords identified easier repossession in this survey is much lower than the proportion of 41% reported in the survey of the landlords of lettings made between 1982 and 1984 (Todd & Foxon, 1987).

14.11 Nearly a third (30%) of lettings had agents who said easier repossession would be the most helpful change to landlords, possibly reflecting the greater extent to which agents, compared with landlords, had experienced problems getting repossession since 1984 (see also Chapter 11).

14.12 Similarly, whereas 8% of lettings had landlords who selected having less troublesome tenants as the most important change, this was selected by the agents of twice as many, 16%, of the lettings.

14.13 Thus nearly half (46%) of the lettings managed by agents had managers who thought that these two changes, related to the management of accommodation (easier repossession, less troublesome tenants), would most help landlords. Only a quarter of lettings (25%) had owners who said this, possibly reflecting the fact that agents were considering their own interests as much as those of their clients in responding to this question.

14.14 Seventeen % of lettings had owners (and 12% of lettings had agents) who said that higher rents would be the most helpful change. This is almost exactly the same as the proportion of lettings made between 1982 and 1984, (16%), whose landlords wanted higher rents (Todd and Foxon, 1987), but much lower than the proportion of all lettings in England in 1976, (47%), whose owners wanted either higher rents (24%), or rents linked to costs (17%) or more frequent reviews of rents (6%) (Paley, 1978).

14.15 Changes which would reduce the levels of tax paid on net rental income, were identified by the landlords of 22% of lettings and the managing agents of 23% as the most helpful change. Smaller proportions of lettings had landlords and managers who wanted less tax on capital gain (6% and 3% respectively) as the most helpful change. However, these proportions are somewhat higher than in previous surveys (Paley, 1978; Todd and Foxon, 1987) and these suggest that, with markets rents now being obtainable in the deregulated sector, landlords were looking as much to the tax system as to the market to assist them with getting the returns that they wanted.

14.16 A small minority of lettings had landlords (10%) and agents (7%) who said that government subsidies or grants would be the most helpful change. The next section shows what forms of financial assistance (whether in the form of tax allowances or subsidies or grants) would be helpful to all landlords.

14.17 Only a very small proportion of lettings had landlords (2%) and agents (four %) who said that having a better public image would be the most helpful change.

14.18 Eleven % of lettings had landlords who said that there were no changes that would help them (only 1% of lettings had agents who had this view). Table 14.3 shows that it was sideline landlords who did not regard their sample letting as an investment and institutional landlords who said that no changes would help. This is confirmed by Table 14.3, which shows that it was lettings owned by growth and income seekers (as well as by slump victims) which had smaller proportions of landlords saying that no changes would help, in contrast to those whose owners let them to employees or for other reasons.

Table 14.3 : The change that would most help landlords by landlords' investment orientation					
	Growth seeker	Income seeker	Slump victim	House employees	Other
	%	%	%	%	%
Less tax on rent income	19	34	8	1	20
Higher rents	22	17	21	9	18
Easier repossession	21	15	25	22	14
Government subsidies or grant	7	7	4	13	4
Less troublesome tenants	7	8	12	12	7
Less tax on capital gain	7	7	12	3	6
Less building control/ environmental health regulation	4	4	-	1	2
A better public image	2	3	4	-	2
Something else	3	2	4	4	1
None	9	2	8	30	16
Not applicable	3	-	-	3	1
Sample number	100	183	24	67	167
Base: all landlords and agents					

14.19 There were two significant differences between types of landlords and these are shown in Table 14.4. First, greater proportions (approximately 3 in 10) of lettings owned by sideline landlords for investment purposes and by business landlords than by other landlords had owners who said that paying less tax on rental income would most help. Second, greater proportions of lettings owned by institutions (24%) than of others had landlords who said that government subsidies or grants would be of most help.

Table 14.4 : The change that would most help landlords by type of landlord

	Type of landlord			
	Sideline sample letting		Business	Institu-tional
	Non-investment	Investment		
	%	%	%	%
Less tax on rent income	15	32	29	-
Higher rents	19	19	16	8
Easier repossession	17	17	17	17
Government subsidies or grant	10	6	6	24
Less troublesome tenants	9	5	12	10
Less tax on capital gain	7	6	8	2
Less building control/ envirnonmental health regulation	1	4	5	3
A better public image	2	3	2	3
Something else	1	2	3	5
None	2	18	3	25
Not applicable	1	2	-	2
Base	103	197	184	59

Base: all lettings where landlord interviewed

14.20 There were no marked differences in the views of landlords with different sized portfolios (Table 14.5). The fact that greater proportions owned by landlords with the largest portfolios said that government subsidy or grant would help, reflects the numbers of these owned by institutional landlords. This is also the reason why a smaller proportion of those in the largest portfolios have landlords who said that less tax on rent income would be of most help.

Table 14.5 : The change that would most help landlords by size of landlords' total lettings portfolio

	Portfolio size (lettings)			
	1	2-7	8-40	41+
	%	%	%	%
Less tax on rent income	25	24	25	14
Higher rents	20	18	15	15
Easier repossession	11	17	24	17
Government subsidies or grant	5	8	8	16

Less troublesome tenants	6	10	6	11
Less tax on capital gain	5	8	8	5
Less building control/environmental health regulation	1	2	4	4
A better public image	4	2	2	2
Something else	1	1	2	5
None	20	8	6	9
Not applicable	1	1	1	2
Base	138	132	120	150

Base: all landlords and agents

14.21 There were significant relationships between landlords' expectations about the sizes of their portfolios over the subsequent two years and what they said about policy change (Table 14.6).

Table 14.6 : The change that would most help landlords' by whether landlords expected their portfolio to change in size

	Increase	Remain the same	Decrease
	%	%	%
Less tax on rent income	24	25	13
Higher rents	13	15	26
Easier repossession	15	17	21
Government subsidies or grant	22	8	6
Less troublesome tenants	4	9	8
Less tax on capital gain	3	6	8
Less building control/environmental health regulation	6	3	2
A better public image	4	3	-
Something else	3	2	3
None	4	12	12
Not applicable	-	1	1
Base	89	312	125

Base: all lettings where landlord interviewed

14.22 Lettings with landlords who expected their total lettings to increase within the next two years had owners who were more likely (22%) than others to say that government subsidies or grants would be the most helpful change. If the lettings were owned by those expecting either their portfolio to increase or to stay the same in size, their owners were more likely (24% and 25% respectively) than those expecting a decline in their lettings (13%) to say that paying less tax on rental income would most help.

14.23   Those lettings whose landlords expected their portfolios to decrease were more likely than others to have owners who said that easier repossession (21%), higher rents (26%) and less tax on capital gains (8%) would most help (or that there would be no changes that could help them as landlords).

14.24   To recap on the most helpful change:

- if landlords expected their portfolio to **increase**, they were more likely than others to want government grants or subsidies and to pay less tax on rent income; they were less likely to want easier repossession, less troublesome tenants and higher rents;

- if landlords expected their portfolio to **decrease**, they were more likely than others to want easier repossession, less troublesome tenants, higher rents and less tax on capital gains and less likely to say that they wanted government grants or subsidies, less tax on rent income, fewer building controls and a better public image.

The most helpful type of financial assistance

14.25   All landlords were asked what would be the most helpful type of financial assistance for them if the government were to provide such help for landlords, both to individuals who were private landlords and to residential property companies. Agents were asked what they thought would be the most helpful assistance to individual and company landlords.

Table 14.7 : The most helpful type of financial assistance by whether landords are individuals or companies/other organisations				
	Interview with			
	Landlords		Agents	
	Individuals	Companie s	Views about individual landlords	Views about company landlords
	%	%	%	%
Exemption from tax on rent income	49	20	62	19
Exemption from tax on capital gains	14	10	8	8
Capital grants for provision of rental property	12	16	14	20
Capital allowances for investment in rental property	5	21	9	22

Revenue grants for the provision of rental property	4	7	2	9
Can't say	13	23	4	22
Not applicable	1	4	<1	1
Base	313	230	210	149

Base: all lettings

14.26 As Table 14.7 shows, there were significant differences between the opinions of individuals and of companies (including all other organisations within this category of companies). This difference was present whether the views were expressed by landlords themselves or whether the views were those of their agents. The discussion therefore concentrates on what the landlords themselves said in response to these questions.

14.27 Lettings owned by individuals were more likely than those owned by companies and others to have owners who said that exemption from tax on rent income would be most helpful. Where landlords themselves were interviewed, the landlords of nearly half the lettings (49%) said this, compared with the owners of only 20% of lettings where the landlords were companies.

14.28 Only 14% of lettings with individuals as landlords had owners who said exemption from tax on capital gains would help most, only slightly greater than the 10% of lettings with companies as landlords whose owners said that exemption from corporation tax with respect to capital gains would most help.

14.29 The next three types of assistance shown on Table 14.7 are about help which would be designed to stimulate provision and investment in rental property.

14.30 Twelve % of lettings owned by individual landlords had owners who said that capital grants would help most (along with 16% of lettings owned by companies and other organisations). Only 5% of lettings with individual landlords had owners who thought capital allowances would help, but 21% of company owned lettings had landlords who said this. Only small proportions of lettings had landlords who said that revenue grants would be the most helpful type of financial assistance.

14.31 To sum up, nearly two thirds of individually owned lettings had landlords who said that exemption from tax on rent or capital gains would most help and only 21% said that capital, revenue grants, or capital allowances would most help. In contrast, only 30% of company owned lettings had landlords who said that exemption from corporation tax would be the most helpful type of financial assistance, whilst 44% had owners who said that grants or capital allowances would help most. Only 13% of lettings had individual owners who decided they could not say what form of assistance would help most, but nearly twice that proportion (23%) of company owned lettings had landlords who said this, possibly reflecting the number of institutions who found it difficult to see how financial assistance would affect them.

Table 14.8 : The most helpful type of financial assistance for individual landlords by type of landlord			
	Sideline sample letting		Business
	Noninvestment	Investment	
	%	%	%
Exemption from tax on rent income	47	48	60
Exemption from tax on capital gains	14	14	11
Capital grants for provision of rental property	9	14	13
Capital allowances for investment in rental property	5	7	-
Revenue grants for the provision of rental property	2	7	4
Can't say	22	7	9
Not applicable	1	1	2
Base	137	131	45

Base: all lettings where individual landlord interviewed

14.32 As Table 14.8 shows, there were few differences in what was regarded as the most helpful type of financial assistance in terms of the type of individual landlord. However two differences should be noted. First, a greater proportion of lettings owned by business landlords than of others had owners who said that exemption from tax on rent income would be the most help. Second, a greater proportion of those owned by sideline landlords for noninvestment purposes than of others had owners who could not say what the most helpful assistance would be.

Table 14.9 : The most helpful type of financial assistance for company or organisation landlords by type of landlord				
	Sidelinesample letting		Business	Institutional
	Non-investment	Investment		
	%	%	%	%
Exemption from tax on rent income	13	26	40	-
Exemption from tax on capital gains	7	9	24	-
Capital grants for provision of rental property	20	28	15	20
Capital allowances for investment in rental property	20	19	14	10
Revenue grants for the provision of rental property	3	7	2	15
Can't say	35	6	3	45
Not applicable	2	4	2	8
Base	60	53	58	59

Base: all lettings where company/organisation landlord interviewed

14.33 There were similar differences as far as landlords who were companies (or organisations) were concerned (Table 14.9). First, lettings with sideline (investment) (26%) and business landlords (40%) were more likely than others to have owners who said that exemption from corporation tax would be the most helpful form of financial assistance. Second, sideline (noninvestment) and institutional landlords were more likely than others to have been unable to say what type of assistance would help most. Broadly similar proportions of lettings owned by all types of landlords had owners who said they would find grants or allowances for provision to be most helpful.

14.34 Finally, Tables 14.10 and 14.11 show that individual and company landlords who expected an increase in their lettings within the next two years identified different types of financial assistance as most helpful in contrast to those expecting either a decline in their portfolio or that it would stay unchanged in size:

- individual landlords expecting an **increase** were more likely than others to say that capital grants would help and less likely to say that tax exemptions would help (Table 14.10);

Table 14.10 : The most helpful financial assistance for individual landlords by whether landlords expected their portfolio to change in size

	Increase	Stay the same	Decrease
	%	%	%
Exemption from tax on rent income	40	48	62
Exemption from tax on capital gains	-	15	15
Capital grants for provision of rental property	37	11	5
Capital allowances for investment in rental property	7	5	7
Revenue grants for the provision of rental property	-	6	9
Can't say	17	14	-
Not applicable	-	1	-
Base	30	213	58

Base: all lettings where individual landlord interviewed

- company landlords expecting an **increase** were also more likely than others to say that capital and revenue grants would most help and less likely to say that capital allowances would help most and that they could not say what would be most helpful (Table 14.11).

Table 14.11 : The most helpful financial assistance for company/organisation landlords by whether landlords expected their portfolio to change in size

	Increase	Remain the same	Decrease
	%	%	%
Exemption from tax on rent income	10	29	5
Exemption from tax on capital gains	8	8	15
Capital grants for provision of rental property	34	13	19
Capital allowances for investment in rental property	12	20	13
Revenue grants for the provision of rental property	12	7	3
Can't say	17	21	28
Not applicable	7	1	6
Base	59	99	67

Base: all lettings where company/organisation landlords interviewed

References

Bevan, M., Kemp, P.A. and Rhodes, D. (1995) *Private Landlords and Housing Benefit*, Centre for Housing Policy Research Report, York: University of York.

Carey, S. (1995) *Private Renting in England 1993/94*, London: HMSO.

Crook, A.D.H. (1986) 'Privatisation of housing and the impact of the Conservative Government's initiatives on low cost home ownership and private renting between 1978 and 1984 in England and Wales: 4. Private renting', *Environment and Planning A*, 18, 1029-1037.

Crook, A.D.H. and Martin, G. (1988) 'Property speculation, local authority policy and the decline of private renting in the 1980s: A case study of Sheffield' in Kemp, P.A., *The Private Provision of Rent Housing*, Aldershot: Avebury, pp.40-77.

Crook, A.D.H., Hughes, J. and Kemp, P.A. (1995) *The Supply of Privately Rented Homes*, York: Joseph Rowntree Foundation.

Crook, A.D.H., Henneberry, J. and Hughes, J. (1996) *Renovations by Private Landlords*, London: HMSO.

Dodd, T. (1990) *Private Renting in 1988*, London: HMSO.

Down, D., Holmans, A. and Small, H. (1994) 'Trends in the size of the private rented sector in England', *Housing Finance*.

Findlay, l., Poynter, R. and Ward, M. (1996) *CPAG's Housing Benefit and Council Tax Benefit Legislation*, London: Child Poverty Action Group.

Ford, J., Kempson, E. and Wilson, M. (1995) *Mortgage Arrears and Possessions; Perspectives from Borrowers, Lenders and the Courts*, London: HMSO.

Forrest, R. and Murie, A. 'Home ownership in recession', *Housing Studies*, 9, 55-74.

Kemp, P.A. (1988) *The Future of Private Renting*, Salford: University of Salford.

Kemp, P.A. and McLaverty, P. (1993) *Rent Officers and Housing Benefit*, Centre for Housing Policy Discussion Paper No. 3, York: University of York.

Kemp, P.A. and McLaverty, P. (1994) 'The determination of eligible rents for housing', *Environment and Planning C: Government and Policy*, 12, 109-122.

Kemp, P.A. and Rhodes, D. (1994) *Private Landlords in Scotland*, Edinburgh: Scottish Homes.

Paley, B. (1978) *Attitudes to Letting in 1976*, London: HMSO.

Rauta, I. and Pickering, A. (1992) *Private Rentin in England 1990*, London: HMSO.

Thomas, A. and Snape, D. (1995) *In from the Cold - Working with the Private Landlord*, London: Department of the Environment.

Todd, J.E., Bone, M.R. and Noble, I. (1978) *The Privately Rented Sector in 1978*, London: HMSO.

Todd, J.E. and Foxon, J. (1987) *Recent Lettings in the Private Rented Sector 1982-84*, London: HMSO.

Zebedee, J. and Ward, M. (1995) *Guide to Housing Benefit and Council Tax Benefit 1995/96*, London: Chartered Institute of Housing and Shelter.

Appendix

Research Methods

The research involved structured interviews with two samples of private landlords. The first sample survey was funded by the Joseph Rowntree Foundation (JRF) and the second by the Department of the Environment. Preliminary results of the JRF funded survey - based on interviews with landlords in Britain rather than just in England - were included in a report on *The Supply of Privately Rented Homes* published by the JRF in March 1995 (Crook, Kemp and Hughes, 1995). The present report draws on both interview samples in order to facilitate a more detailed analysis of the data.

Sampling

There is no readily available sampling frame for private landlords. The only feasible way of obtaining statistically reliable data about the people and organisations that let private housing is to obtain their names and addresses from a representative sample of private tenants. The JRF sample of landlord addresses was obtained from private tenants interviewed in the OPCS monthly Omnibus Survey; the sample for the DoE sample was obtained from tenants interviewed by OPCS in the Survey of English Housing. Both the Omnibus Survey and the SEH sample of households are drawn monthly by OPCS from the Postcode Address File. The subsequent interviews of landlords were conducted by SCPR using a questionnaire designed by the authors of this report.

The *OPCS Omnibus Survey* is based on a representative sample of the adult population (aged 16 or over) in Great Britain. Approximately 2000 interviews are carried out each month. The response rate is normally in the range 75-80% (after exclusion of ineligible addresses). Over an eight month period from February 1993 to September 1993, interviewees that were heads of household or their spouse were asked for the name and address of their landlord. (The proportion of households in the interviewed sample that are heads of household or their spouse is usually between 82% and 85%.) If the respondent was unable to give this information, they were asked if the landlord used a managing agent for their property, and if so, the name and address of the agent was sought.

These OPCS Omnibus private tenant respondents were given a letter from the University of York explaining the nature of the research and provided with assurances regarding the confidentiality of the information to be given by landlords.

The *Survey of English Housing* (SEH) is a based on a representative sample of the adult population living in England. Approximately 2250 interviews are carried out each month, with a response rate (net of ineligible addresses) of 80-85%. Over a fifteen month period from April 1993 until June 1994, private tenant heads of household or their spouse who were interviewed in the SEH were asked to give the name and address of their landlord (or failing that, of the managing agent).

As with the Omnibus survey, the SEH private tenant respondents were given a letter from the Department of the Environment explaining the nature of the research and providing assurances about the confidentiality of the information to be given by landlords. Unlike the JRF sample, however, they were also told that their name and address would not be passed on to the survey firm; as discussed later, this had an important consequence for the address about which information was sought from landlords.

198

Response

In total 72% of Omnibus Survey private tenants gave information about their landlord; the remainder were either unwilling to pass on details or did not know their landlord's name or address. This yielded an unclustered sample of 600 names and addresses of landlords and agents. After removing addresses that proved to be out of scope, interviews were carried out in December 1993 and January 1994 with the landlords of 347 addresses in Great Britain (of which 301 were in England), a response rate of 75%. Of the landlord interviews in England, 212 (70%) were with landlords and 89 (30%)with managing agents.

In total, 65% of eligible SEH respondents provided information about their landlord in respect of 817 addresses. Interviews were subsequently carried out during August and September 1994 with the landlords of 547 privately rented addresses, a response rate (after excluding out of scope addresses) of 78%. Of these interviews, 334 (65%) were with landlords and 181 (35%) with agents.

Obtaining a sample of private landlords via private tenants in this way means that the survey provides information about *the landlords of a representative sample of privately rented addresses*. Hence the sample numbers used to calculate the percentages in the tables of the report are based on addresses and not on landlords. To illustrate this point, the figure of 61% in Table 2.1 should be read to mean that 61% of PRS addresses had a landlord that was a private individual; and not that 61% of landlords were private individuals. This distinction is important because many landlords own more than one letting. Hence if the tables had been calculated as a percentage of landlords it would mean that landlords with more than one letting would be under-represented in the data.

Sample validation

OPCS were commissioned by DoE to carry out a validation exercise to ascertain the representativeness of the achieved landlord sample derived from the SEH survey. Three sets of comparison were carried out: (i) differences between those who were willing to provide their landlord's name and address and those who declined; (ii) for those who gave names and addresses, differences between those whose landlord was interviewed and those whose landlord was not interviewed; and (iii) differences between tenants whose landlord was interviewed and all other tenants. The range of tenant variables which were used for these comparisons included age, sex, ethnic group, income, type of tenancy, type of accommodation, rent, and relationship with the landlord. Because many of these variables are inter-related a statistical technique known as logistic regression was employed in order to assess the independent affect of each variable on the likelihood of tenants providing landlord information and achieving a successful interview.

The conclusion of this validation analysis by OPCS was that there was little evidence of bias in the sample between tenants who provided landlord details and those who did not, between tenants whose landlord was interviewed and those whose landlord was not interviewed, and between landlords who were interviewed and those who were not. Tenants who provided landlord details were more likely to consider their rent high and less likely to rent from a private individual than those who did not provide details. Tenants whose landlords were interviewed tended to have higher rents (£30 per week or more) than other tenants. There was no evidence that tenants who were on poor terms with their landlord or who were dissatisfied with their accommodation were under-represented in the landlord sample.

The questionnaire

In both samples, there were two separate but compatible versions of the questionnaire, one for landlords and the other for agents. There were minor wording differences to reflect the difference between the two types of respondent, but otherwise the questions were the same in both versions. However, the agent questionnaire was a shorter version of that used for the landlord interviews; questions which it was felt that agents would not necessarily be in a position to answer were excluded. The questionnaire used for both the JRF and the DoE samples were the same, except that ten additional questions - about difficulties, information needs, sources of advice, and court action - were added to the DoE one.

The questionnaires were in two parts. The first part comprised questions which were about a specific privately rented address, while the second part was made up of questions about the landlord's (or agent's) views and experience of letting accommodation more generally.

One crucial difference between the two surveys, however, was that only in the case of the JRF sample were the property specific questions asked about the privately rented address that had come up in the sample of tenants. In the DoE sample, because (as mentioned above) the tenant was informed that their address would not be passed onto the survey firm, it was not possible to ask the landlord (or agent) about the sampled address; to get around this problem, landlords and agents were asked about the address at which they had made their most recent letting.

Because of this difference, it is possible to combine the data from the two surveys only in respect of the questions which were about the landlord's views and experiences in general and not those which were specific to the property. The property specific questions in the JRF survey are therefore based on a representative sample of privately rented addresses, while those in the DoE survey are based on the recent lettings of the landlords of a representative sample of privately rented addresses. We have referred to the former as the *all lettings* sample and the latter as the *recent lettings* sample.

Other DoE Research on the Private Rented Sector

■ **In from the Cold: Working with the Private Landlord**, DoE, 1995, (£15.50), ISBN 185112239 7. Available from Publication Sales Unit, Block 3, Spur 7, Government Buildings, Lime Grove, Eastcote, Ruislip, Middlesex, NA4 8SF. Tel. 0181 429 5186/7. A summary of this research is available from Room N7/12, Social Research Division, Department of the Environment, 2 Marsham Street, London SW1P 3EB. Telephone: 0171 276 3223

■ **Private Renting at the Crossroads: an Economic Analysis of Rent Determination in the Private Rented Sector in England**, Coopers and Lybrand 1995. Available from John Hawksworth, Coopers and Lybrand, 1 Embankment Place, WC2N 6NN. Tel. 0171 583 5000.

■ **Housing in England 1994/95: Survey of English Housing**, HMSO 1996 (£30), ISBN 0 11 691672 9. This has a chapter on private renting, which includes the size and characteristics of the sector, the types of letting, rents, Housing Benefit, and income and rent. Available from HMSO publications centre. Tel. 0171 873 9090

■ **English House Condition Survey 1991**, HMSO 1993 (£35), ISBN 0 11 752880 3. This profiles the characteristics and use of the housing stock (all tenures), it's facilities and services and condition. Available from HMSO publications centre. Tel. 0171 873 9090

■ If you wish to know more about the Department's research about landlords or the private rented sector, please contact Jan White on 0171 276 3258

Printed in the United Kingdom for HMSO
Dd302100 7/96 C10 G559 10170